Ken Yeang

Eco Skyscrapers

Ken Yeang

Eco Skyscrapers

Ivor Richards (Editor)

images
Publishing

Third edition published in Australia in 2007 by
The Images Publishing Group Pty Ltd
ABN 89 059 734 431
6 Bastow Place, Mulgrave, Victoria 3170, Australia
Tel: +61 3 9561 5544   Fax: +61 3 9561 4860
books@imagespublishing.com
www.imagespublishing.com
The Images Publishing Group Reference Number: 743

Printed by
Everbest Printing Co. Ltd., in Hong Kong/China

First Edition published in 1994 by
Artemis London Limited

Second Edition published in 1998 by
Ellipsis London Limited

Contact

T . R . Hamzah & Yeang Sdn. Bhd. (Company No. 41743A)
No.8 Jalan 1, Taman Sri Ukay
Off Jalan Ulu Kelang, 68000 Ampang
Selangor, Malaysia
[tel] 00 603 4257 1966   [fax] 00 603 4256 1005
[email] trhy@trhamzahyeang.com

Llewelyn Davies Yeang
Brook House,
Torrington Place,
London   WC1E 7HN   UK
[tel] 44 0 20 7637 0181   [fax] 44 0 20 7637 8740
[email] info@ldavies.com

Websites
www.trhamzahyeang.com
www.ldavies.com

The information and illustrations in this publication
have been prepared and suppiled by
ADF Management Sdn Bhd (Co.No.15884-V,Malaysia).

ISBN 978 1 86470 268 2

Contents

Preface

Sustainability or the green agenda is today irrevocably embedded at the heart of the UK's political, statutory, legislative environment, and now is increasingly influencing its financial environment. Conferences, seminars, exhibitions and expert reports on 'sustainability' and 'green' issues proliferate, as those in the property development world seek to understand the nature of the environmental debate and to find their respective roles and responses.

Most of the UK's major cities, including London, Birmingham, Liverpool and increasingly its secondary cities and conurbations such as Brighton, Bristol and Croydon, are now experiencing an unprecedented interest in tall buildings, and some within locations that would have previously been regarded as sacrosanct. The political justification for the tall building lies in the recognition of its potential in delivering sustainable planning and design solutions to the UK's inner cities. Within this context, the Mayor of London, Ken Livingstone personally sought to champion significant changes to London's skyline to accommodate both the demands of international financial interests and the intensifying pressure to provide solutions to high-density living, especially on underused brownfield sites.

Such has this new found interest in the tall building been that the UK government's own design watchdogs, the Commission for the Built Environment (CABE) and English Heritage (EH), have jointly published key design guidance on tall buildings. The guidance seeks to provide an intelligent framework for the public to respond to the imminent pressures of building skywards, especially where development is taking place on sensitive urban sites.

Ken Yeang's undisputed leadership in the design of ecoskyscrapers, evident over his last three decades of work, is already well known. These signature 'deep green' tall buildings flow in his blood. His inspirational work started from our now sister firm, Hamzah & Yeang which has produced several benchmarking tall buildings; many of these are award winning high-rises, notably in the Asia region. Also of great importance are his numerous treatises and monographs defining the bioclimatic (and now advancing to the ecological) skyscraper, which cast their own enlightened shadows upon today's eco-politico-design agendas.

His joining us to become Llewelyn Davies Yeang (LDY) (in 2005) was synergistic with our company's reputation within the UK's local Authorities for having widely influenced the national agenda on sustainable planning. Interestingly, our company (before Ken) had been responsible for the tallest hospital building in the world - the Queen Mary Hospital in Hong Kong, working with David Scott of Arup Engineering, as well as the recently completed UK's tallest hospital building at the University College London Hospital.

The simultaneous confluence of the global proliferation of tall buildings with the current debate on climate change provides fertile ground for Ken. Many of LDY's new projects lie within temperate and cold climate zones (including those that fall below 25°C), and which are now being designed across Europe, Asia and North America. This exciting evolution in his work will no doubt attract close observations and critical reviews by his peers over the next several years as his new formal and aesthetic responses create a new 'deep green' vertical architecture. An important part of Ken's work is the inherent desire to constantly innovate in all respects (in theory, technical systems, methodologies, built form and aesthetics, etc.) - this ensures that these new projects inherit a pioneering quality as well as a signature status from an architect who, above many others, truly understands the deepest meanings of designing to reduce the causes of climatic change and environmental impairment, and at the same time advancing ways to design the tall building type.

This book presents indisputable evidence of Ken's depth of knowledge and experience in the field of designing ecoskyscrapers and moreover presents the great excitement and sheer delight that these increasing hybrid structures of his manifest.

Steve Featherstone
Managing Director
Llewelyn Davies Yeang

Foreword

In 2007, for the first time ever, more than half the world's population will be living in an urban habitat. With the population doubling every 65 years, and the continuing flow of people from the rural to the urban environment, it is perhaps not surprising that we are in the midst of a global construction boom, one that may last for some time. To keep up with the changing demographics, new accommodations will be required for an overwhelming 100 million people each year in the foreseeable future. The pressure on urban land values and the need for urban densification to accommodate this growing population is evident. High-rise construction is one of the few ways that cities can expand while improving their urban connectivity and functionality.

So what form will these high-rise towers of the future take? The towers will undoubtedly be sustainable, since the last decade has seen a multifaceted and almost universal commitment to green design. However, sustainability as a design process is in its infancy: there is much to be done to define it and to differentiate it from "greenwash". For this reason, Ken Yeang's inspiring book about his vision for the future of eco and bioclimatic skyscrapers is both welcome and timely, and describes a radical alternative to conventional box towers.

Ken provides a challenging and invigorating look at what can be achieved, when design is approached from a strictly bio-climatic perspective. Using external climate and the environment as the main drivers of the form, plan and building orientation, Ken has created a series of buildings that are exceptional and have a unique and active relationship to their surroundings. In his book he describes a range of techniques to create low energy-use buildings with passive control systems. He seeks to create a natural environment for the building occupants and in the process creates elegant, aesthetic design solutions and buildings that seem to belong to their location.

Ken's concepts are very appealing to me because of the interesting and unusual forms he creates and because of his drive to reduce energy consumption in towers. Complex geometry has always interested me as an engineer, but as leader of the Council on Tall Buildings and Urban Habitat I am most concerned about the large amounts of energy used in tall buildings and what we can do to change our current approach. Energy conservation is being tackled on many fronts, particularly in the design of tall buildings where the potential to save energy is so great. However, despite the fact that buildings today consume about half of the world's energy, there is very little hard data on how much energy any particular building uses. So neither designers nor the public will know if they are living and working in a gas-guzzler or in a hybrid type building. It is like someone designing a car engine without any mileage measurements. Legislation in Europe will shortly mandate collecting this data and several cities in the US are also looking at collecting this data for major projects. When this data becomes available it will radically change the way tall sustainable buildings are designed and operated, and will encourage innovative and radical approaches to low energy buildings, such as those described in Ken Yeang's book.

For thirty years Ken has been a tireless advocate for low energy buildings and has combined that with a passion for tall buildings. His distinctive approach to tall building design uses climatic conditions such as sun-paths, local and prevailing wind flow patterns, ground and building temperature ranges as well as site access and environment conditions to determine the form of the building. Ken was doing this long before it became fashionable. In this book he comprehensively describes his design philosophy and illustrates it with sketches and diagrams from a range of designs and from his completed buildings.

Ken Yeang seeks to create his energy efficient buildings through basic design. Almost every element of his plans has many functions, from the cores that act as solar shield to the sun shades that act as wind scoops or collect rainwater for re-use. His designs seek to maximise the amount of natural daylight, natural ventilation and natural vegetation and through his sleek sculpting, he creates a series of user friendly spaces with extensive terraces and planting, windows that open, shade devices that protect the occupants from the hot summer sun and large clear facades that face the north horizon. His buildings are designed to connect the occupants to their environment and he argues very clearly, that, in doing this, a natural reduction in energy use will ensue; people do not want to insulate themselves from their natural environment but rather prefer to connect with it.

Although some of Ken's buildings appear to be quite complex, they were built for commercial clients and had the normal commercial restrictions and cost limitations. It is quite remarkable that several of his buildings, including the wonderful award winning, Menara Messinga building, were completed more than 10 years ago, when designers were much more restricted in what they could do than they are today. Ten years later these buildings are still at the forefront of the green movement, and the Menara Messinga building is still one of the most authentic expressions of a tropical skyscraper. Recent technological advances will make it much easier to achieve buildings of a similar or even greater complexity.

This book will be an inspiration for all designers that seek to build sustainable skyscrapers.

David M Scott
Council on Tall Buildings and Urban Habitat's Chairman

Introduction

A review of Ken Yeang's architecture at Llewelyn Davies Yeang and earlier at Hamzah & Yeang should be seen in the context of architectural history, and the earlier work of Wright, Neutra and Schindler, together with the more recent output of Foster, Rogers and Piano. Equally designers such as Victor Papanek and economist-prophet Fritz Schumacher all have established positions and principles relevant to Yeang's agenda. The seminal influence of Buckminister Fuller, as inventor-architect, should also be acknowledged, as Yeang's response to region, programme, climate and context – relative to his agenda for sustainability – has encompassed the thought and principles of all these figures. But, it is the single-minded action and commitment in the area of bioclimatic and ecological design that has made Yeang's architecture significant, and his collaboration with creative engineers that has enabled much of his work to be achieved.

Just as Yeang's work should be rightly set in a global context in terms of both history and development in 20th century architecture, equally his projects for tall buildings should be seen as a constantly developing series, and not as isolated, sensational events. What is on hand, is the emergence of an appropriate and responsive architecture for the 21st century – a sustainable architecture based on ecological principles.

In order to exemplify this architectural response, a limited set of four of his skyscrapers are taken here as a representative range of Yeang's more recent works, although these are only part of a much larger collection that this book incorporates. The four projects include the Tokyo-Nara Hypertower 1993, the Singapore EDITT Tower 1998, the Kuala Lumpur BATC Tower 1997-99, and the Penang UMNO Tower 1995-98. However, in order to properly locate these projects in relation to Yeang's overall works and context, it is essential to first mention the benchmark tower, Menara Mesiniaga, realised between 1989-92 in Kuala Lumpur, for IBM's Malaysian agency.

Menara Mesiniaga, a 15 storey landmark office tower, is essentially configured within a circular plan form and marks the culmination of Yeang's sunpath projects. The cylindrical form is deeply incised by a series of spiralling sky courts, which develop into three-story atria with terraces at the higher levels. These spiralling recessions are heavily planted, beginning from a splayed berm at the base, which houses entrance and computer facilities. The skycourts and atria assist the channelling of cool airflow throughout the transitional spaces of the offices and the planting provides both shade and an oxygen-rich environment. The service cores are gathered into a solar shield-tower on the east façade, while the west face is protected by sun-shading. The cores, containing the lifts, stairwells and restrooms, are naturally ventilated with day-lit spaces. The office skycourts and terraces also provide release to the exterior and natural ventilation when required.

The curtain-glazed north and south walls are a response to the tropical over-head sunpath, moderating solar gain and augmenting the natural day-lit office spaces, which encircle the peripheral plan, with conference facilities forming an inner core. The roof-level swimming pool and gymnasium are covered by an outrigger structure, which provides a site for the future addition of photo - voltaic solar cells. The project also incorporates systems management to reduce energy consumption by all equipment, including air-conditioning plant.

Although there is precedent in Yeang's earlier work, Menara Mesiniaga is the archetypal summary of the bioclimatic sun-path type, which exhibits the clear principles of solar-shielding and orientation, coupled with the insertion of planted skycourts and atrial recessions. Details such as sun-shading spandrels, and size and profile of protective are all subjected to precise geometrical arrangement related to sun angle and path, while the materials specification throughout is related to studies of embodied energy. The external form is appropriately dominated by the spiraling planting of the courts and atrial spaces that are the signal of Yeang's bioclimatic architecture, which is significantly low-energy in operation. At the same time, the building exploits the quality of the pleasant tropical climate, uniting office workers with the natural environment. The bioclimatic skyscraper thus stands as an exemplar and in sharp contrast to the sealed, air-conditioned, centrally cored and energy-consumptive form of its essentially North American counterpart.

The four towers represent progressive developments within the range of Yeang's bioclimatic series. Tokyo-Nara Supertower is essentially a spiraling form, rotating within a controlling circular geometry, which extends several theoretical propositions. The Singapore EDITT Tower and the Kuala Lumpur BATC Tower are both signature forms, displaying freer organic plan arrangements that incorporate ideas for vertical urbanism. While these are not built, the fourth project for the Pulau Pinang UMNO Tower was completed in 1998 and essentially wind wing-walls, applied to a constrained rectilinear plan, are the central innovation. This series also demonstrates Yeang's designs as a progression from formal geometry to a freer organic expression. The formal progression is matched by an expanding ecological and urbanistic investigation.

TOKYO-NARA HYPERTOWER 1993

This is a project that both extends and experiments with several theoretical ideas founded in earlier works, in particular that of Menara Mesiniaga, Kuala Lumpur 1992. Both Mesiniaga and Nara tower forms are constrained within the outline of a circle and contain the principle of a vertical spiral of boundless dimensions. While the KL Mesiniaga Tower is a mere 15 storeys, the Nara Tower can be visualized and extended to 210 storeys or 880 metres high, almost double the vertical dimensions of Pelli's Petronas Towers in Kuala Lumpur. The Nara Tower project provided Yeang with the opportunity to realize and expressively confirm many of his theoretical ideas. This project represents a summary of his research to 1993, "… into the nature and evolution of tall buildings …"

The central ideas in the project design and its conception are dominated by the spiral floor-plate structure festooned with vertical landscaping, which loops around and penetrates the form and its progression of vertical spaces. This is a direct development of the Mesiniaga principle, and in the same way the abundant foliage assists in cooling the building mass. Equally, the planted fringes of floors and atrial spaces contribute to the control of air movement within the overall structure. In this case the calculated, assembled mass of planting balances the biosystems with the mechanical systems in a symbiotic relationship that yields a stable environment – a bioclimatic machine a habité. In response to the maintenance needs of the vertical landscaping, glazing and panel cladding systems, Yeang introduced an innovative robot-arm as a form of 'cherry picker' on movable trellises. These traveling devices move on an external track that spirals the tower in vertical, expressive circulation.

The structural system is a tour de force: a three-point equilateral triangle defines a tripartite primary cellular honeycomb structural frame, linked and set within the circular geometry of the robot track system. This matrix provides a support system for the radial/spiral arrangement of organic floor plates (described as plectrum shaped). As the floor plates are rotated at alternative floors, the overlapping layers provide a natural shading system. This shifted pattern allows the introduction of hanging gardens, inter-floor bracing, ventilation and cooling system networks. The main structure is penetrated centrally by a pivotal cable stay mast, and this element, together with the outer triple V-form structures, define the positions for batteries of vertical transportation. The floor plate spiral shift also creates variations of atrial space that are further infused with terraces, internal courts, private gardens and sky courts.

Throughout, Yeang envisaged his first principles of vertical urbanism. These included principally: mixed occupancy such as offices, apartments, hotel and communal facilities; skycourt oases, the equivalent of green parks; and the atrial spaces as a public areas of movement, vistas, air and light. The skycourt oases, located at regular vertical intervals, provide major breaks in the built volume – a form of suspended natural park, introducing fresh air and acting as the Tower's lungs, distributing via the atrial voids an essential airflow while insulated from the city beneath. The atrial network of spaces, winding within the tower, provides a sheltered interaction of walkways, bridges and stairwells – a pedestrian system of routes, open to the environment but particular to the tower itself. Taken together with the central core, these elements provide an overall system of wind-flues, which bring wind to inner parts of the building, with adjustable dampers. This principle has been further developed in the wind wing-wall system used in the Penang UMNO Tower.

As with the Mesiniaga Tower, the lift and service cores are laid defensively on the east - west axis of the sunpath to absorb the maximum quantity of solar gain. The cooler facades on the north - south axis are conversely, more open with clear glazing and atrial voids, echoing the earlier precedent. In the same bioclimatic tradition the shielding and glazing systems are oriented to resist solar gain. The east - west facing sides are more solidly glazed, with acts and perforated metal cladding selected for qualities of reflection, weight and structural capacity. And again, the north - south faces of the form are equally legible by the open louvres, tiered sunshades and clear glazing in response to the lower exposure to the sun.

The vast spiral form of this bioclimatic supertower is intended to rise independent of the polluted lower city beneath, reaching into the inhabitable upper atmosphere, in Yeang's words "…at the edge of the sky". Armoured against solar gain and strategically opened to introduce natural ventilation, the overall spatial composition and functional mix offers the possibility of a new form of urban life. Where it to be realized, Yeang would doubtless add to the design many further principles developed in later projects such as rain irrigation, ecosystem hierarchy, recycling and embodied energy assessment. In its present form as an earlier project (1993) it remains both as an iconic statement, and as the key link between the diminutive Mesiniaga Tower and the current series of super towers which Yeang has been subsequently engaged. As the scale of the projects increases, the ecological design agenda expands.

SINGAPORE EDITT TOWER 1998

The design for the EDITT Tower, on a site owned by the Urban Redevelopment Authority (URA) for an urban corner in Singapore, is a hybrid form. In its current state it fulfils the client's programme requirements for an Exposition Tower, but the nature of its design formation allows future transformation to offices or apartments.

The 26-storey tower project, situated at the junction of Middle Road and Waterloo Street, is remarkable in two principal respects. First, the design advances Yeang's ideas for a civilized vertical urbanism – the continuous extension of street life into the elevated levels of the skyscraper. Second, Yeang uses the project to explore and demonstrate his consolidated ecological approach to tower design. This involves an even wider agenda than that he has applied in earlier projects. Finally, the design and its inherent plan geometry displays a freer, organic composition – related both to public space and circulation – and therefore marks a departure from the KL Mesiniaga and Tokyo-Nara Towers, whose forms are controlled within a circular plan particularly towards a new ecological aesthetic. The overall programme of uses is defined by the nature of an Expo event and includes retail areas, exhibition spaces and auditorium uses as well as more conventional open office spaces on the upper levels, which are adaptable.

The controlling V-form structural geometry is evident in the plan from level 1 above ground, but the three-dimensional form does not express this clearly until level 12. This is largely due to the inclusion of groups of pedestrian ramps, which alternate, within the vertical progression from the north to the south faces of the tower. At level 20 to level 30, the ramp systems are so extended that they occupy the whole western sector of the plan, between the north and south faces extending an expressive principle of public circulation that is similarly first signaled at the introductory levels between ground, and level 1 through to 3.

Otherwise, the plan organization reveals the signature hallmark of Yeang's designs. These include vertical landscaping, here further developed; skycourts, atrial spaces and plazas; and very heavy solar-shielding of the eastern face, with a cranked, unified 'wall' of stairtowers, lifts and restroom accommodation.

The two central propositions of place making and public circulation, coupled with an extended ecological agenda both take their place as major forces and expressive elements within the design. They are the root and content of the whole architectural form, whose elegant inflection has resulted in a design of great freedom and substance. In addition, Yeang's approach here substantiates his earlier statement, that "… the design of energy-efficient enclosures has the potential to transform architectural design from being an uncertain, seemingly whimsical craft, into a confident science". It is also delivering a new, environmentally responsible version of the modernist canon, where sociable openness and climate informs its essential spatiality.

Yeang has made a crucial point in the design of the Editt Tower in that the major issue in the urban design of skyscrapers, "… is poor spatial continuity between street-level activities with those spaces at the upper - floors of the city's high-rise tower …" in the conventional case, which is based on repetitious, physical compartmentalisation of floors within an inherently sealed envelope.

Yeang's central manifesto is that urban design involves 'place making'. In the Editt Tower he has applied this principle with conviction. "... in creating 'vertical places', our design brings 'street-life' to the building's upper - parts through wide landscaped - ramps upwards from street - level. Ramps are lined with street activities: stalls, shops, cafes, performance spaces and viewing decks, up to the first six floors. Ramps create a continuous spatial flow from public to less public, as a 'vertical extension of the street', thereby eliminating the problematic stratification of floors inherent in the tall buildings typology. High-level bridge - linkages are added to connect to neighbouring buildings for greater urban connectivity."

In addition to the consideration of public space and circulation, Yeang added an analysis of views to enable upper-floor design to have greater visual connectivity with the surroundings. In Singapore, with its superb seaboard location, this is a significant factor, and rightly exploited.

But, it is the manipulation and integration of the ramp, within the form and function of the project, that emerges as the fundamental precept of the architecture and its manifestation of public space and use. In common with the early projects of Le Corbusier, and more recently Richard Meier, the ramp is once again celebrated here as a symbolic notation, and the visible expression of the promenade architectural.

Aside from the abundant, spiraling landscape of indigenous vegetation which assists ambient cooling of the façade, two further elements appear foremost in the form-giving process. These include the curvilinear rooftop rainwater collector, and the attendant rainwater façade collector scallops, which form the rainwater collection and recycling system. Equally the extensive incorporation of photovoltaic panels, as a major formation on the east façade, adds a further level of formal detail residual in the overall bioclimatic discipline, towards reduced energy consumption.

In this case, Yeang's ecological response begins with an extensive analysis of the site's ecology. This exhaustive analysis of ecosystem hierarchy, determines that this site is an urban 'zero-culture'. Consequently, this is a crucial determinant, which focuses the design approach towards the restoration of organic mass, which will enable ecological succession to replace the inorganic nature of the site, in its current urban state of devastation.

This policy is manifest in the planted façades and terraces of the project, which are continuously ramped upwards from the ground plane to the roof-summit level and constitute a significant proportion of planted to useable floor area. Yeang included a survey of indigenous planting within a 1 mile radius of the site in order to select species that will not compete with those already present in the locality. Sustainability underscores every move.

Otherwise, Yeang's ecological design process includes a further series of significant analyses. Perhaps most important is to submit the project to a 'loose-fit' philosophy, which will enable the building to absorb change and refitting over a life-span of 100 - 150 years. Overall, this allows conversion from the expo-condition to possible office use, with a high level of floor occupation efficiency. This involves removable partitions and floors, reuse of skycourts, mechanical jointing, which enable future recovery of materials, all within a matrix that is based upon flexibility as a paramount condition.

In addition, Yeang introduced a series of systems and assessment procedures that further underscore the ecological design of the tower. As well as water recycling and purification associated with rainwater and grey-water reuse, the project includes sewage recycling, solar energy use, building material's recycling and reuse, together with natural ventilation and 'mixed-mode' servicing. The latter optimizes the use of mechanical air - conditioning and artificial lighting systems are reduced, relative to the locality's bioclimatic responses. Ceiling fans with demisters are used for low-energy comfort cooling. Wind is also used to create internal comfort conditions by the introduction of 'wind-walls', that are placed parallel to the prevailing wind to direct airflow to internal spaces and skycourts, to assist breeze cooling.

Finally, the whole material fabric and structure of the tower were subjected to an embodied energy and CO_2 emission assessment, in order to understand the environment impact of the project, and to define a balance between embodied and operational energy content. While these methods are neither unique nor overly new in themselves, it is the coordinated collective effect of their application in Yeang's architecture that signals his ecological attitude to design, and provides the basis for development in his following projects.

BATC SIGNATURE TOWER 1997

In order to describe the Signature Tower adequately it is essential to place it in the context of the overall development to which it belongs, as a key component. The Business Advancement Technology Centre forms a massive mixed-urban development, incorporating some university faculties on a site in Germany.

As an integrated urban masterplan, the project represents one of the largest proposals Yeang has designed, and opens the opportunity to demonstrate the principles of his bioclimatic approach applied to the design of tall buildings, and larger high - technology urban village with transportation structure. The 47 acre site is envisaged as a landscaped park within which the buildings are placed and serviced by a central series of public plazas, boulevard walkways and controlled car access routes. The rapid transit system (LRT) forms a central spine with a station at the mid-point junction between retail, commercial and university facilities.

The site is divided, therefore, into three zones. A central north - south zone of the major public spaces and activities, edged on the east and west by two further fluid parkland areas into which the array of facilities are inserted and attached to the central V-form spine. The 60-storey Signature Office Tower and the five, 30-storey office towers are sited within the parkland areas, as part of this ensemble.

As landscaping is applied to the entire development, the whole immense project viewed from the peripheral roads is seen as a grand park with the buildings located and immersed within this natural setting. The towers are accessed via the mounted landscaped ground plane of the site, while water gardens and soft landscaping are introduced to enhance the pedestrian routes throughout the site in general. Many of the routes provide weather-protected, semi-covered pedestrian circulation, free of vehicular intrusion. This is a principle, that has its origins in Yeang's earlier work, such as his conceptual proposals for the Tropical Verandah City of 1987.

Related to the overall principles of a landscape concept, landscaped and terraced skycourts have been incorporated at intervals in the office tower floors as they ascend, providing both an amenity for relaxation, and a continuous visual and physical linkage, threading together all storeys. The vertical urbanism, in this case, accords with a vertical ascension of public gardens and parks. This concept is further supported with Yeang's incorporation of public places in the sky – the amenities of a traditional city, but vertically located in the tower forms. In all six towers for the BATC Masterplan, the principles Yeang employed for the Singapore EDITT Tower are first enacted into a major exposition of the bioclimatic skyscraper. In turn these tall buildings all incorporate integrated Building Management Systems to control internal conditions by monitoring sensors located on the roof – effectively Yeang's version of a bioclimatic weather station.

The significance of the BATC Towers lies in the fact that they exist as a part of a much larger idea, centred on a harmony of bioclimatic principles, and framed within the urban master plan, as a whole. The BATC center and Branch Campus of UTM contains a School of Advanced Education Programmes in high technologies catering for 5000 students. This is coupled with industry, research and development centers for 20 institutions, in order to advance business opportunities arising from the research. The associated High-Technology Office Park houses companies involved in the advanced technology industry, including IT and multimedia, and provides these occupants with the shared use of super-capability computer facilities as a basis for a significant center of innovation. The master-plan also incorporates major convention and exposition centers, information and resource centers and a Multimedia and IT College. Each of these facilities occupies either a linked edge site or a part of the spinal arrangement. Further public facilities include a major theme mall for retail entertainment and recreation via multimedia applications; residential blocks to house students, researchers and office workers and a four-star hotel for visitors and tourists, with fully equipped business centers.

All this diverse provision is underscored by the system of public parkland within the site, whose lush greenery and landscape contributes towards an environment that enables high business activity and related research endeavors. A main boulevard system structures the site in vehicle-free conditions that encourage public use with covered pedestrian walkways, or the alternative of an air-conditioned Internal Rapid Transit System, which provides movement within the site, with links to the outer LRT system of the city.

The 60-storey Signature Office Tower is the singular landmark, vertical event of the BATC Masterplan, counterbalanced by the horizontal mass and spaces of the central plaza and spinal facilities. The Signature Tower occupies a central site on the western parkland of the project, with longer sides of its cranked rectilinear plan facing north and south, and the eastern face typically solar shielded with service cores, elevators and restroom clusters.

The sunken lower levels incorporate escalator banks serving the center of the form up to level 4. Above level 32, two systems of pedestrian ramps alternate on the outer north and south faces up to level 40, reducing to the south face only from level 48 through to 60. As with the Singapore EDITT Tower, these ramp formations are an important part of the building's expression of public circulation and the notion of vertical urbanism, seen as a hierarchy within the tower form. Otherwise, the dominant composition elements are the two massive vertical landscape parks occupying a large area of the atrial voids and skycourts at the higher levels. These are augmented by a ramping park at the base, and ten other smaller parks distributed over the height of the building's section.

As the central and most prestigious flexible office facility for the whole development, the innovative bioclimatic design offers a first - class daily environment for its occupants. The intermissions of restaurants, sky - plazas and special gallery spaces, with the overall development of the vertical gardens, park and extensive skycourt voids, taken together, mark Yeang's most flamboyant tower project of his current series. On another level, much of the technical innovation of the Singapore EDITT Tower could be expected to appear, when the project is ultimately realised.

The Signature Tower summarises Yeang's vision of the Skyscraper as the Vertical City - in - the - Sky. This is primarily achieved through the vertical coupling of multiple programmes of space use, within the overall programme of the tower as a spatial construct. This idea is then further emphasised by a three - tier hierarchy of circulation systems, and the system of vertical landscaping, parks and squares both ascending and cross - cutting the overall form. The singular force of the concept is perhaps best conveyed in Yeang's coloured elevational notations of his tripartite vision.

Beyond the tower itself, however, the most significant impact of the total masterplan is the application of bioclimatic principles to the overall urban design of the BATC complex, regardless of type.

PENANG UMNO TOWER 1995-98

The UNMO Tower is one of a series of projects that Yeang developed and built between 1992 - 98, using slim rectilinear plan forms on dense urban site locations. These projects include Central Plaza, and the Budaya Tower, both in Kuala Lumpur and realised between 1992 - 96. While all these towers were designed within the framework of Yeang's bioclimatic agenda, the UMNO project for downtown Penang is singularly distinguished by its concentration on natural ventilation and the development of wind wing-walls in this connection.

The thin elongated urban site-plan of the tower is situated at the junctions of Jalan Zainal Abidin and Jalan Macalister, resulting in the extended longitudinal facades being exposed to a south - east or north - west orientation. This is often a function of such valuable urban-land locations.

The 21-storey tower design responds with a virtually solid solar shield - wall of elevators, staircases and restrooms with service cores, as in Yeang's other bioclimatic projects. In this case the shield wall not only protects the critical south - eastern face from solar gain, but its projecting planar terminals, at the north and sough extremities, form two of the wind wing - walls that are particular to the natural ventilation strategy of the project and its office spaces.

The base of the UMNO Tower contains a deeply recessed, double - height banking hall, together with the glass - canopied main entrance raised on a shallow podium and accessed from Jalan Macalister, the main thoroughfare. The base also contains the main plant spaces and car - ramps that give access to parking areas in level 2 through level 5. Level 6, the principal occupied floor, houses an auditorium for meetings and assemblies. Above this rise, 14 floors of office floor space for let. Several floors, such as level 9 and level 12, have extensive break - out roof terraces, and the roof levels are shielded by a steel structured, elevated shade canopy.

The solar shield - wall accommodation of elevator lobbies and restrooms are naturally sun-lit and ventilated, and typically accord with Yeang's low - energy agenda. Similarly, all office floors, although designed to be air - conditioned, can be naturally ventilated. The thin plan - form, of each floor - plate, means that no desk location is more that 6.5 metres distant from an openable window, enabling all office users to receive natural sunlight and ventilation. Although the project was originally designed for tenants to install their own split unit air - conditioning, due to expected low rental rates in Penang, ultimately a central air - conditioning system was installed. The design for natural ventilation, in its realized form, thus provides a back-up system for the building, in the event of power - failure. Major sun - shaded installations on the curvilinear north - west office wall are solar orientated, and outrigged shield - shades are provided to the car park floors, also on this façade.

But, it is the wind wing - wall system, which in this case dominates the streamlined form of the UMNO Tower architecture, and it is perhaps significant that Yeang has persistently compared the vertical - scale of the building, to the aerofoil form of one to a one and a half times the length of a typical jumbo - jet aircraft. The symbolic inference of building-airstream - aircraft, and the cross - referencing of the sophisticated serviced shell, has long existed in Yeang's essays and in certain projects, such as this, comes closer to a transferable vision.

The architect's own notes on the development of the wind wing - wall design are of significance, as they describe his system of research and application, "The building has wind wing-walls to direct wind to special balcony zones that serve as pockets with air - locks, having adjustable doors and panels to control the pecentage of openable windows, for natural ventilation. This building is probably the first high-rise office (tower) that uses natural ventilation for creating comfort conditions inside the building… For internal comfort as in this building, a higher level of air - change per hour is required. Here, we tried to introduce natural ventilation at point of entry, rather than create suction at the leeward side. To create pressure at the inlet, a system of 'wing - walls' to 'catch' the wind from a range of likely directions (are introduced). The wing - walls are attached to a balcony - device with full-height sliding - doors. The placements of the wing - walls and air - locks within the floor plate are based on the architect's assessment from the locality's wind - data. The wing - wall cum air - lock device is of course, experimental, and site verification with CFD analysis indicates that this device worked reasonably well. Experience from the project, will enable the architect to further develop the device for other projects."

And this has indeed been the case, for the design of the Editt tower for Singapore uses the same principles to create internal comfort conditions, by the incorporation of 'wind - walls' as an integral device, in the natural ventilation strategy in a sequence, but they also point up the process which informs his architectural expression - a process that allows functional low-energy design to bring sophisticated form to what would otherwise be just an office tower, in the conventional sense. In creating the bioclimatic skyscraper, Yeang has not just evolved a new type, but has developed both low - energy architecture and the spatiality of vertical urbanism.

Further it has been said of Yeang's work, that:
"… his towers as they ascend in Kuala Lumpur or Penang or Ho Chi Minh City seem, in their paradoxical mix of orders and desires, to achieve a synthesis exactly appropriate to the cultural promise of South - East Asia, their warrior-like stance ready for the economic revolutions of the new century ".

The fact that Ken Yeang has brought about his sustainable architecture, and its range of achievements, within a harsh commercial environment, in itself is commendable, but even more important is the fact that his work and the improved environments his buildings offer, has affected the quality of life for countless occupants for the better.

Emeritus Professor Ivor Richards
School of Architecture Planning & Landscape, University of Newcastle UK

On Green Design

• Right at the outset, we should be clear that the skyscraper is not an ecological building type. In fact it is one of the most un-ecological of all building types. The tall building over and above other built typologies uses a third more (and in some instances much more) energy and material resources to build, to operate and eventually, to demolish. It is regarded here as a building type that if inevitable, needs to be made ecological in as much as possible.

Its unecologicalness is of course largely due to its tallness which requires for instance greater material content in its structural system to withstand the higher bending moments caused by the forces of the high wind speeds at the upper reaches of its built form, greater energy demands to transport and pump materials and services up the building's floors working against gravity, additional energy consumption for the mechanised movement of people up and down its elevators, and other enhanced aspects arising from its excessive verticality.

What is the rationale for the skyscraper typology and why make it green? The argument is simply that the tall building is a building type that will just not go away overnight and until we have an economically viable alternative to it, the skyscraper as a building type will be with us for a while and will continue to be built prolifically, particularly to meet rapidly the demands of urban and city growth and increasing rural-to-urban migration.

The fundamental truth is simply that it can never be a truly green building, certainly not in totality. If we accept this premise and its inevitable ubiquity, then green designers instead of negating it, should seek to mitigate its negative environmental impacts and to make it as humane and pleasurably habitable for its inhabitants as possible.

There might of course be conditions where its built form might possibly be justifiable for instance to urgently meet needed intensive spatial accommodation and where it is built over or near a transportation hub to reduce transportation energy consumption, and where by virtue of its smaller footprint will have considerably lesser impact on sensitive vegetated greenfield sites or on arable productive land.

• Saving our environment is the most vital issue that humankind must address today. Designing ecologically is thus fundamentally crucial.

Within this context it must also be clear that the building of green and ecological buildings is simply just one part of the entire environmental equation that we must address. We must ultimately change our cities into green ecocities in entirety as well as change all of our industries and manufacturing, all of our forms of transportation and all of the myriad of our human activities. In making these green we must integrate them benignly and seamlessly with the natural environment.

This addressing of the current state of environmental impairment has to be carried out at all levels of our human world globally, regionally, locally and individually.

Change has also to be physically at our built environment, but also at the political level by devising and implementing green legislatures and at the social level in redefining the way we live our lives, all with ecologically benign strategies.

We need new social, economic and political models with non-polluting manufacturing and industrial production proceses, using green systems and materials, that are carbon neutral and with zero-waste as it is with the ecosystems in nature.

Discussed here are some of the key principles and means to design the skyscaper builtform as a human-made ecological system. The principles and ideas here while discussed with regard to the tall building typology, are applicable for the wider role of the redesigning of our human built environment and its physical - social - political - economic systems.

•   The ecological approach to design is about environmental bio-integration. Simply stated, if we are able to integrate everything we do and make in our built environment (which by definition consists of our buildings, facilities, infrastructure, products, refrigerators, toys) with the natural environment in a seamless and benign way, then there will be no environmental problems whatsoever.

This is of course easier said than done. Successfully achieving this then is our challenge.

Ecodesign is designing for bio-integration. This can be achieved in three aspects: physically, systemically and temporally.

•   We start by looking at nature. Nature without humans exists in stasis.

To achieve this similar state of stasis in our human built environment, our built forms and systems need to imitate nature's processes, structure and functions, as in its ecosystems. How can we design our built systems to be like ecosystems?

For instance, ecosystems have no waste. Everything is recycled within.

Thus by imitating this function, our built environment will produce no wastes. All its emissions and products will be continuously reused, recycled within and when emitted are reintegrated benignly with the natural environment. In tandem with this is an increasing efficient use of non-renewable energy and material resources.

This designing to imitate ecosystems is ecomimesis. This is the fundamental premise for ecodesign. Our built environment must imitate ecosystems in all respects. This is what our tall building built form must do.

•   Nature regards humans as one of its many species. What differentiates humans is their capability to force large-scale devastative changes to the environment. Such changes are often the consequences of manufacturing, construction and other human activities (e.g. recreation and transportation).

•   Our built forms are essentially enclosures erected to protect us from the inclement external weather, enabling some activity (whether residential, office, manufacturing or warehousing) to take place.

In this regard, the tall building is an intensification and extrusion of an enclosural system within a comparatively small site footprint. On occasions such small footprints can contribute to ecologically preserve the land within the site for productive uses and in other conditions can contribute positively to preserving and enhancing local biodiversity.

Ecologically, a building is a high concentration of materials on a location (often using non-renewable energy resources) extracted and manufactured from some place distant in the biosphere, transported to that location and fabricated into a built form or an infrastructure (e.g. roads and drains), whose subsequent operations bear further environmental consequences and whose eventual after-life must be accommodated. The skyscraper is in effect, a significantly intensive concentration upon a very small footprint.

- There is also much misperception about what is ecological design today.

We must not be misled and seduced by technology. There is the popular perception that if we assemble in one single building enough eco-gadgetry such as solar collectors, photo-voltaics, biological recycling systems, building automation systems and double-skin facades, we will instantaneously have an ecological architecture.

The other misperception is that if our building gets a high notch in a green-rating system, then all is well.

Of course, nothing could be further from the truth. Worse, a self-complacency sets in whereupon nothing further is done to improve environmental degradation.

Although these technological systems are relevant experiments, perhaps, towards an ecologically responsive built environment, their assembly into one single building does not make it automatically ecological.

- In a nutshell, ecodesign is designing the built environment as a system integrated within the natural environment. The system's existence has ecological consequences and its sets of interactions, its inputs and outputs as well as all its other aspects (such as transportation, etc.) over its entire life cycle, must be benignly integrated with the natural environment.

- Ecosystems in the biosphere are definable units containing both biotic and abiotic constituents acting together as a whole. From this concept, our businesses and built environment should be designed analogously to the ecosystem's physical content, composition and processes. For instance, besides regarding our architecture as just art objects or as serviced enclosures, we should regard it as artifacts that need to be operationally and eventually integrated with nature.

- As is self-evident, the material composition of our built environment is almost entirely inorganic, whereas ecosystems contain a complement of both biotic and abiotic constituents, or of inorganic and organic components.

Our myriad of construction, manufacturing and other activities are, in effect, making the biosphere more and more inorganic, artificial and increasingly biologically simplified. To continue without balancing the biotic content means simply adding to the biosphere's artificiality, thereby making it increasingly more and more inorganic. Exacerbating this are other environmentally destructive acts such as deforestation and pollution. This results in the biological simplification of the biosphere and the reduction of its complexity and diversity.

We must first reverse this trend and start by balancing our built environment with greater levels of biomass, ameliorating biodiversity and ecological connectivity in the built forms and complementing their inorganic content with appropriate biomass.

In the case of the skyscraper which by virtue of its dense built form is already a high intensification of inorganic mass, the integration of the biotic component in an ecological nexus is crucially essential to the skyscraper's built form.

- We should improve the ecological linkages between our designs and our business processes with the surrounding landscape, both horizontally and vertically. Achieving these linkages ensures a wider level of species connectivity, interaction, mobility and sharing of resources across boundaries. Such real improvements in connectivity enhance biodiversity and further increase habitat resilience and species survival.

Providing ecological corridors and linkages in regional planning is crucial in making urban patterns more biologically viable.

Besides improving connectivity and nexus horizontally in our built environment, this linkage must now be extended vertically within the skyscraper's builtform with organic connectivity stretching upwards within the built form to its roofscape, as a form of vertical landscaping.

- More than enhancing ecological linkages, we must biologically integrate the inorganic aspects and processes of our built environment with the landscape so that they mutually become ecosystemic. This is the creation of human-made ecosystems compatible with the ecosystems in nature.

By doing so, we enhance human-made ecosystems' abilities to sustain life in the biosphere.

- Ecodesign is also about discernment of the ecology of the site. This is the first consideration in designing the ecoskyscraper. Any activity from our design takes place with the objective to physically integrate benignly with the ecosystems and the ecology of the locality.

Particularly in site planning, we must first understand the properties of the locality's ecosystem before imposing any intended human activity upon it. Every site has an ecology with a limiting capacity to withstand stresses imposed upon it, which if stressed beyond this capacity, becomes irrevocably damaged. Consequences can range from minimal localised impact (such as the clearing of a small land area for access), to the total devastation of the entire land area (such as the clearing of all trees and vegetation, leveling the topography, diversion of existing waterways). This is the physical integration of our built system with the natural environment.

In most instances, skyscrapers are built on zero-culture land, or land whose ecology has already been cleared or built over and extensively modified. The ecological benefit of the skyscraper built form is its small footprint which has lesser impact on the site's ecology, and if the site remains vegetated (and not all entirely paved) it provides greater land area for surface water percolation back into the earth.

•   To identify all aspects of this carrying capacity, we need to carry out an analysis of the site's ecology.

We must ascertain its ecosystem's structure and energy flow, its species diversity and other ecological properties. Then we must identify which parts of the site (if any) have different types of structures and activities, and which parts are particularly sensitive. Finally, we must consider the likely impacts of the intended construction and use.

•   This is, of course, a major undertaking. It needs to be done diurnally over the year and in some instances over years. To reduce this lengthy effort, landscape architects developed the 'layer-cake' method, or a sieve-mapping technique of landscaping mapping. This enables the designer to map the landscape as a series of layers in a simplified way to study its ecology.

As we map the layers, we overlay them, assign points, evaluate the interactions in relation to our proposed land use and patterns of use, and produce the composite map to guide our planning (e.g. the disposition of the access roads, water management, drainage patterns and shaping of the built form(s)).

•   Designing the ecoskyscraper also involves configuring its built form and operational systems as low-energy systems that are non-dependant (in totality or as much as possible on non-renewable sources of energy). Ecomimicry tells us that like ecosystems its only source of energy has to be from the sun. Designing for temporal integration is about designing for the long term sustainable use of the biosphere's renewable and non-renewable resources.

In addressing this, we need to look into ways to create internal comfort conditions within the tall building built form as low energy design. There are essentially five modes: Passive Mode (or bioclimatic design), Mixed Mode, Full Mode, Productive Mode and Composite Mode, the latter being a composite of all the preceeding.

Designing for low energy means looking first at Passive Mode strategies first, then Mixed Mode to Full Mode, Productive Mode and to Composite Mode, all the while adopting progressive strategies to improve comfort conditions relative to external conditions while minimising demands on non-renewable sources of energy.

Passive Mode design is bioclimatc design, or designing to optimise on the ambient energies of the locality by designing with its local climate and seasonal variations. A quick indicator of the locality's climatic conditions is its latitude. Of course, even within a given latitude there are wide climatic variations, dependant for instance on whether it is an inland site or by the waterfront or its altitude above sea level.

Meeting contemporary expectations for comfort conditions cannot be achieved by Passive Mode or by Mixed Mode alone. The internal environment often needs to be supplemented by using external sources of energy, as in Full Mode.

Full Mode uses electro-mechanical systems or M&E (mechanical and electrical) systems to improve the internal conditions of comfort, often using external energy sources (whether from fossil-fuel derived sources or from local ambient sources).

Ecodesign of our buildings and businesses must minimise the use of non-renewable sources of energy. In this regard, low-energy design is an important objective.

Passive Mode is designing for improved comfort conditions over external conditions without the use of any electro-mechanical systems. Examples of Passive Mode strategies include adopting appropriate building configurations and orientation in relation to the locality's climate, appropriate façade design (e.g. solid-to-glazed area ratio and suitable thermal insulation levels, use of natural ventilation and use of vegetation.

The design strategy for the built form must start with Passive Mode or bioclimatic design. This can significantly influence the configuration of the built form and its enclosural form. Therefore, this must be the first level of design consideration in the process, following which we can adopt other modes to further enhance the energy efficiency.

Passive Mode requires an understanding of the climatic conditions of the locality, then designing not just to synchronize the built forms design with the local meteorological conditions, but to optimise the ambient energy of the locality into a building design with improved internal comfort conditions without the use of any electro-mechanical systems. Otherwise, if we adopt a particular approach without previously optimizing the Passive Mode options in the built form, we may well have made non-energy-efficient design decisions that will have to correct with supplementary Full Mode systems. This would make nonsense of designing for low-energy.

Furthermore if the design optimises its Passive Modes, it remains at an improved level of comfort during any electrical power failure. If we have not optimised our Passive Modes in the built form, then when there is no electricity or external energy source, the building may be intolerable to occupants.

The location of the elevator core in the configuring of the skyscraper's built form can contribute to its low energy performance by serving as a thermal buffer between the inside of the internal spaces with the external environment.

• Mixed Mode is where we use some electro-mechanical (M&E) systems. Examples include ceiling fans, double facades, flue atriums and evaporative cooling.

• Full Mode is the full use of electro-mechanical systems, as in any conventional building. If our users insist on having consistent comfort conditions throughout the year, the designed system heads towards a Full Mode design.

It must be clear now that low-energy design is essentially a user-driven condition and a life-style issue. We must appreciate that Passive Mode and Mixed Mode design can never compete with the comfort levels of the high-energy, Full Mode conditions.

• Productive Mode is where the built system generates its own energy (e.g. solar energy using photo - voltaics, or wind energy).

Ecosystems use solar energy, which is transformed into chemical energy by the photosynthesis of green plants and drives the ecological cycle. If ecodesign is to be ecomimetic, we should seek to do the same. At the moment the use of solar energy is limited to various solar collector devices and photovoltaic systems.

In the case of Productive Modes (e.g. solar collectors, photovoltaics and wind energy), these systems require sophisticated technological systems. They subsequently increase the inorganic content of the built form, its embodied energy content and its use of material resources, with increased attendant impacts on the environment.

Ideally as in ecosystems, we should use energy-generation systems that imitate photosynthesis (e.g. photovoltaics using dye-cells).

• Composite Mode is a composite of all the above modes and is a system that varies over the seasons of the year.

• Ecodesign also requires the designer to use green materials and assemblies of materials, and components that facilitate reuse, recycling and reintegration for temporal integration with the ecological systems.

We need to be also ecomimetic in our use of materials in the built environment. In ecosystems, all living organisms feed on continual flows of matter and energy from their environment to stay alive, and all living organisms continually produce wastes. As mentioned earlier, an ecosystem generates no waste, one species' waste being another species' food. Thus matter cycles continually through the web of life. It is this closing of the loop in reuse and recycling that our human-made environment must imitate.

We should unceremoniously regard everything produced by humans as eventual garbage or waste material. The question is what do we do with the waste material?

If these are readily biodegradable, they can return into the environment through decomposition, whereas the other generally inert wastes need to be deposited somewhere, currently as landfill or pollutants.

Ecomimetically, we need to think about how the skyscraper's components and its outputs can be reused and recycled at the outset in design before production. This determines the processes, the materials selected and the way in which these are fabricated, connected to each other and used in the skyscraper built form.

For instance, to facilitate reuse, the connection between components in the skyscraper's builtform needs to be mechanically joined for ease of demountability. The connection should be modular to facilitate reuse in an acceptable condition.

•   Another major design issue is the systemic integration of our built forms and its operational systems and internal processes with the ecosystems in nature.

This integration is crucial because if our built systems and processes do not integrate with the natural systems in nature, then they will remain disparate, artificial items and potential pollutants. Their eventual integration after their manufacture and use is only through biodegradation. Often, this requires a long-term natural process of decomposition.

While designing for recycling and reuse within the human-made environment relieves the problem of deposition of waste, we should integrate not just the inorganic waste (e.g. sewage, rainwater runoff, wastewater and food wastes, but also the inorganic ones as well.

•   We might draw here an analogy between ecodesign and prosthetics in surgery.

Ecodesign is essentially design that integrates our artificial systems both mechanically and organically, with its host system being the ecosystems. Similarly, a medical prosthetic device has to integrate with its organic host being the human body. Failure to integrate well will result in dislocation in both.

By analogy, this is what ecodesign in our built environment and in our businesses should achieve: a total physical, systemic and temporal integration of our human-made, built environment with our organic host in a benign and positive way.

•   Discussed here are some of the key issues to help us approach the ecological design of the skyscraper to be ecologically responsive, and to bio-integrate its built form and its systems with the natural environment.

Ken Yeang
London

Typology of Plans

Editt Tower

Tokyo-Nara Tower

Chong Qing Tower

Menara Boustead

Palomas 2 Tower

Al-Ghorfa Tower

Beijing WSTC Tower

BATC Tower

Elephant & Castle Tower

Ho Chi Minh City Tower

IBM Plaza

National Library Building

Shanghai Armoury Tower

Idaman Residence Tower

MAAG Tower

Al-Asima Tower

The Residence Tower

The Plaza Tower

Menara UMNO

EXPO 2005 Tower

Yee Nen Tower

Reliance Tower

Four Seasons Hotel Tower

Gnome Research Building

Typology of Plans

Buildings & Projects

EDITT Tower

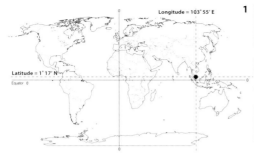

1

Location
Singapore

Climatic Zone
Tropical

Vegetation Zone
Rainforest

No. of Storeys
26

Areas
GFA   : 3,771 sq.m.
NFA   : 3,567 sq . m.

Site Area
838 sq.m.

Plot Ratio
1:4.5

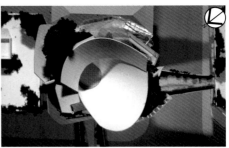

2

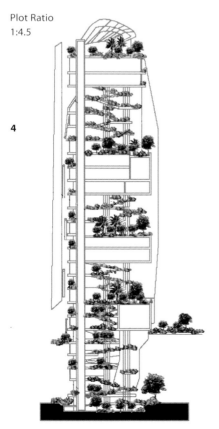

4

3

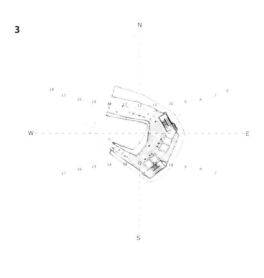

The tower is on a typical city centre 'zero culture' site which is a devasted urban ecosystem that has none of its original top soil, flora and fauna remaining. The design response biologically rehabilitates the site's almost entirely inorganic character with a well-planted façade with garden terraces in the form of a continuous 'landscaped ramp' that weaves its way upwards from the ground plane to the summit of the tower.

The continuous vegetated areas occupy a surface area of biomass that equals approximately half the gross area of the entire tower, in an exceptionally high ratio of abiotic to biotic components in this human-made ecosystem.

The selection of the new planting species is derived from a survey of the locality's existent ecology such that the species introduced will not compete with those that are existent and not endanger the locality's biodiversity.

The planting contributes to the ambient cooling of the façades through evapo-transpiration.

The landscaped ramp coupled with the continuously shifting organic plan form results in built form that is literally a vertical landscape.

5

6

7

Legend
1 Site plan
2 View from south
3 Sun path diagram
4 Cross-section
5 Worm's eye view
6 South - east elevation
7 South elevation

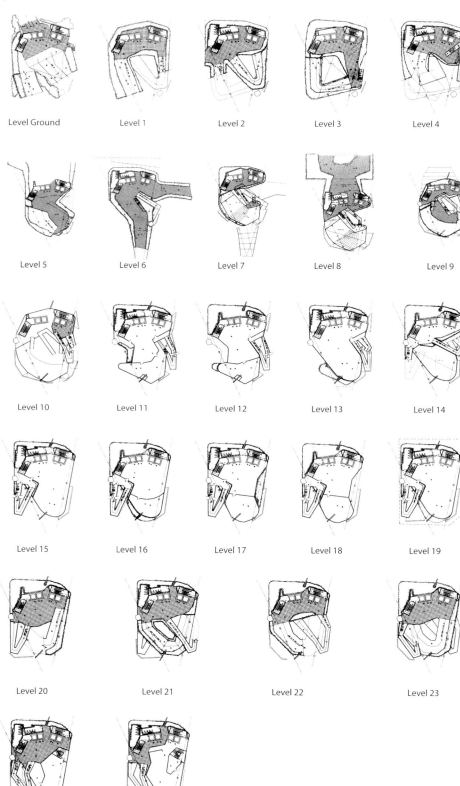

Level Ground

Level 1

Level 2

Level 3

Level 4

Level 5

Level 6

Level 7

Level 8

Level 9

Level 10

Level 11

Level 12

Level 13

Level 14

Level 15

Level 16

Level 17

Level 18

Level 19

Level 20

Level 21

Level 22

Level 23

Level 24

Level 25

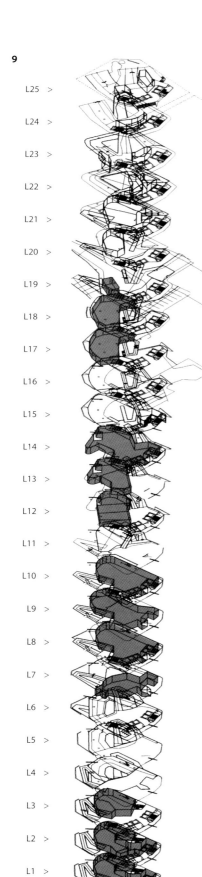

L25 >

L24 >

L23 >

L22 >

L21 >

L20 >

L19 >

L18 >

L17 >

L16 >

L15 >

L14 >

L13 >

L12 >

L11 >

L10 >

L9 >

L8 >

L7 >

L6 >

L5 >

L4 >

L3 >

L2 >

L1 >

Legend

8 Summary of plans

9 Axonometric diagram

10 Landscaped ramp

11   Planting Concept

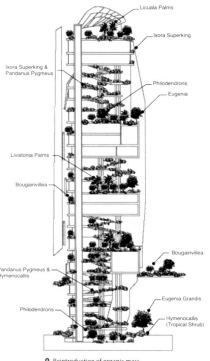

Licuala Palms

Ixora Superking

Ixora Superking & Pandanus Pygmeus

Philodendrons

Eugenia

Livistonia Palms

Bougainvillea

Bougainvillea

Pandanus Pygmeus & Hymenocallis

Eugenia Grandis

Philodendrons

Hymenocallis (Tropical Shrub)

Reintroduction of organic mass to an urban locality to encounter balance inorganic nature of the site.

12   Rainwater Gravity Filtration System

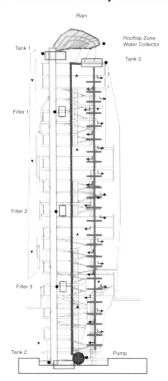

Rain

Tank 1

Rooftop Zone Water Collector

Tank 3

Filter 1

Filter 2

Filter 3

Tank 2

Pump

13   Rainwater Collection and Recycling

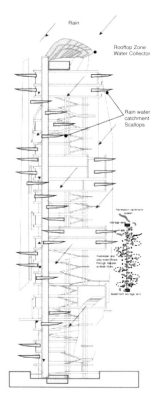

Rain

Rooftop Zone Water Collector

Rain water catchment Scallops

14   Solid Waste Recycling

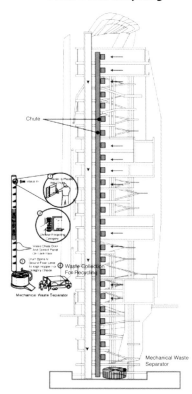

Chute

Waste Collection For Recycling

Mechanical Waste Separator

Mechanical Waste Separator

15

Legend

11 Planting concept
12 Rainwater gravity filteration system
13 Rainwater collection and recycling
14 Solid waste recycling
15 Aerial view

Tokyo-Nara Tower

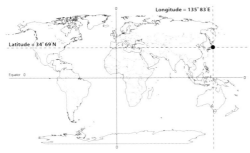

Latitude = 34° 69 N
Longitude = 135° 83 E
Equator 0

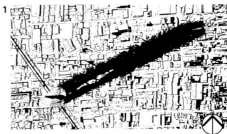

1

2

Location
Tokyo - Nara

Climatic Zone
Cold

Vegetation Zone
Deciduous Forest

No. of Storeys
156

Areas
GFA   : 448,536 sq.m.
NFA   : 313,674 sq.m.

Site Area
Site footprint 22,500 sq.m.

Plot Ratio
1 : 20

4

3

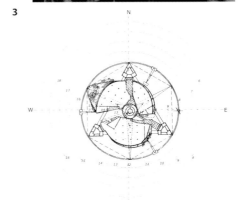

This is a proposal for an ecologically responsive hyper-tower. The tower is an extension of the park-in-the-sky idea.

The design can be summarized as the 'architecture of a hollow rotating vertical spiral' using a system of shifting vertical landscaping terraces.

These intermediate roof - gardens, service a mixed-use occupancy that includes commercial use, offices, hotels, serviced apartments and a variety of residential accommodation.

Most visually apparent is the vertical landscaping which spirals around not just externally but through and within the built form.

This component of the built form performs a number of key functions. The verdant foliage protects the building by way of shading in the summer. By photosynthesis it creates a healthier microclimate at the façade.

The fringing of the floors and the atrial spaces further reduces the impact of high wind speeds on the built structure.

The ratio of the mass of planting relative to the built structure is favourably comparable, thereby ensuring that the biosystems components are balanced and acting symbiotically with the structure's mechanical and electrical systems as an artificial ecosystem.

Located at regular intervals are larger garden skycourts that provide inhabitants with green 'breaks' in the built structure.

These mini green parks, located high above the city are maintained by a number of external cherry-pickers that run on an external spiralling track that is part of the building's management system.

The greenery in the built form act as its lungs, breathing life into the floors above and below via the internal atrial voids.

Legend
1 Site plan
2 Detail of upper floors
3 Sun path diagram
4 Cross-section
5 Elevation

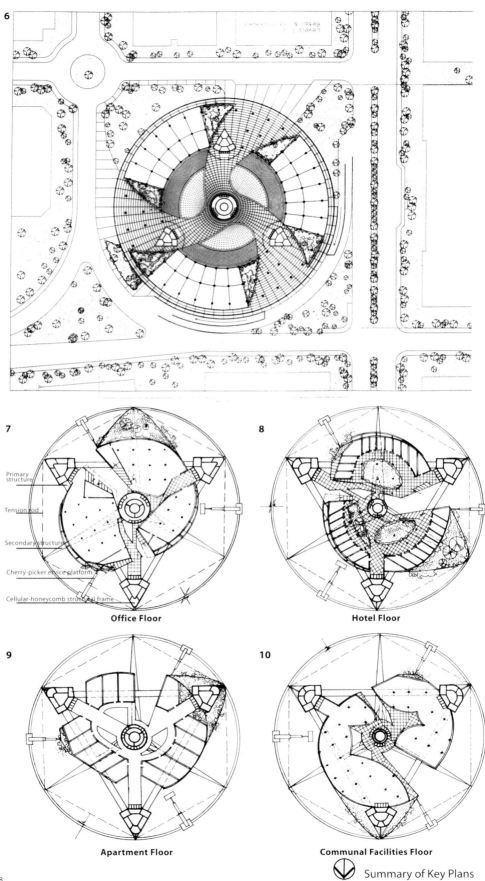

6

7
Primary
structure
Tension rod
Secondary structure
Cherry-picker service platform
Cellular-honeycomb structural frame

Office Floor

8

Hotel Floor

9

Apartment Floor

10

Communal Facilities Floor

Summary of Key Plans

11

1. Seasonal Changes

2. Climate Predictability
Climate is a complex interaction of the atmospheric forces of radiation, air movement and atmospheric pressure. Near the sun's face, micro climatic forces become less predictable

3. Solar Radiation
As the sun's ray passes through the atmosphere its energy is reduced. However, as it hits the cloud level it is reflected, intensifying radiation towards the tower at lower levels.

4. Rainfall
Clouds precipitate water which falls to the ground. As it falls some is lifted by rising air currents and some is evaporated so that its intensity is reduced.

5. Speed of Climatic Change
The ground provided a source of thermal inertia, moderating sudden climatic variations

6. Humidity
Humidity varies throughout the year, however it is the greatest at ground level and within cloud cover.

7. Air Temperature
Air temparature drops with height.

8. Air Density
The density of the atmosphere reduces with height.

9. Ground Noise
Street noise, for example is less noticeable beyond five storeys.

10. Concentration of Polution
The main sources of pollutants are from vehicles and industry. Vehicles deposit more pollutants at ground level, where as industry deposits it at high level.

11. Wind Velocity
The friction of the earth's surface and building reduce airflow.

12. Air Pressure
As the density decreases with height, so does its pressure.

13. Torsion and Wind Forces
Wind forces twist the tower. The torsion is greatest at the base where the tower is restrained, reducing with height.

14. Bending Stresses due to horizontal wind loads
Wind forces bend the tower. The bending stresses are greatest at the base where the tower is restrained, reducing with height.

15. Horizontal shear force due to wind load
Wind forces genarate shear stressess, which the tower accomodates towards its base where the shear forces are the greatest.

16. Axial column load
Column collect the floor loads as they descend the tower.

17. Views
Surrounding buildings at low level obstruct views. At higher level cloud cover will also reduce visibility.

18. Vertical Movement
The movement of people increases towards the entrance at the base of the building.

19. Horizontal Sway
As the wind passes around the tower, the pressure disbalance causes the tower to sway.

20. Horizontal Deflection
As the wind hits the tower it deflects. The greatest deflection is the futherest point from the support at the ground.

Tokyo-Nara Tower

Legend

6 Ground floor
7 Office floor
8 Hotel floor
9 Apartment floor
10 Communal facilities floor
11 Tower features diagrams
12 Height comparison

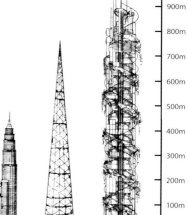

12

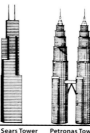

| **Landmark Tower** Yokohama (295m) | **Empire State Building** New York (381m) | **La Tour Sans Fins** Paris (419m) | **Sears Tower** Chicago (457m) | **Petronas Towers** Kuala Lumpur (450m) | **Millenium Tower** Japan (800m) | **Tokyo-Nara Tower** Tokyo Nara (880m) |

900m
800m
700m
600m
500m
400m
300m
200m
100m

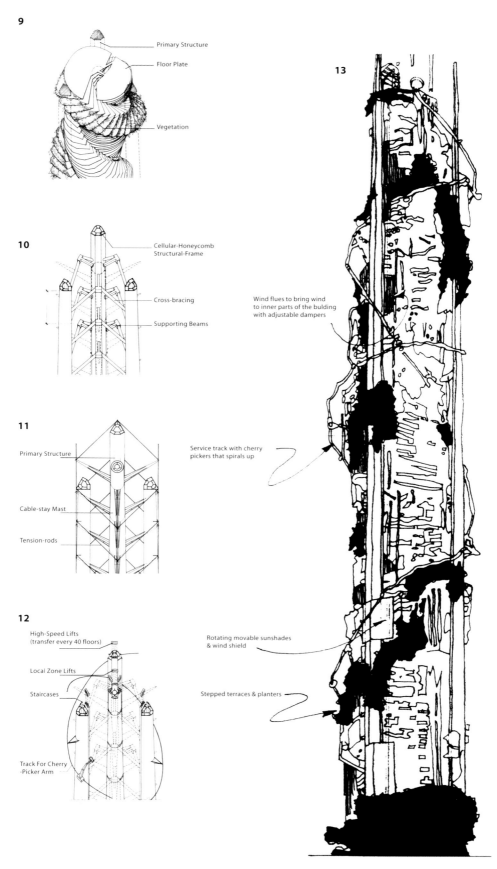

9

Primary Structure

Floor Plate

Vegetation

10

Cellular-Honeycomb
Structural-Frame

Cross-bracing

Supporting Beams

11

Primary Structure

Cable-stay Mast

Tension-rods

Service track with cherry
pickers that spirals up

Wind flues to bring wind
to inner parts of the bulding
with adjustable dampers

13

12

High-Speed Lifts
(transfer every 40 floors)

Local Zone Lifts

Staircases

Track For Cherry
-Picker Arm

Rotating movable sunshades
& wind shield

Stepped terraces & planters

14

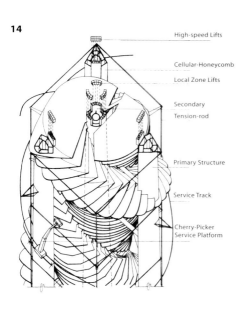

High-speed Lifts

Cellular-Honeycomb

Local Zone Lifts

Secondary
Tension-rod

Primary Structure

Service Track

Cherry-Picker
Service Platform

15

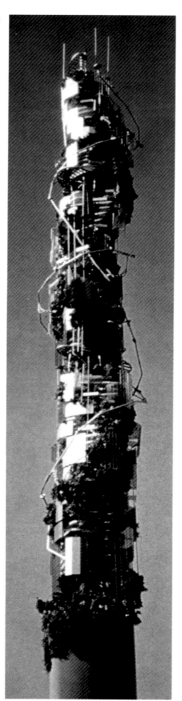

Legend

9 Floor plates stacking
10 Primary structure
11 Secondary structure
12 Vertical circulation
13 Tower features
14 Structure and circulation
15 Elevation

Chongqing Tower

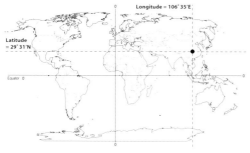

Location
Chongqing

Climatic Zone
Temperate

Vegetation Zone
Alpine

No. of Storeys
22

Areas
GFA   : 25,000 sq.m.
NFA   : 18,900 sq.m.

Site Area
225,412 sq.m.

Plot Ratio
1:9

1

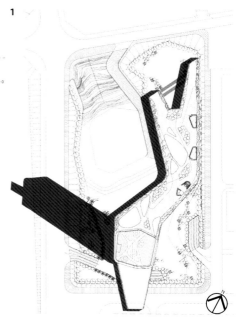

2

4

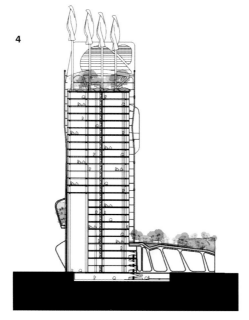

3

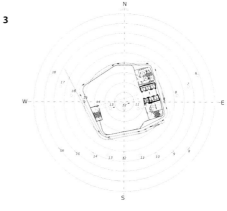

The tower is conceived as a vertical extension of the roof garden of the exhibition hall. A spiral planter system encircles the tower bringing vegetation to the summit.

The site edge is planted with hardy trees and plant species indigenous to Chongqinq with the landscaping continuous from street level to the office tower.

A number of Eco-Cells as vertical cellular slots are integrated into the exhibition hall podium with a spiralling vegetated ramp that starts from the basement up to the roof garden of the podium to bring biomass, vegetation, daylight, rainwater and natural ventilation into the inner depths of the floors.

This vertical landscaped ramp is supported by the external eco-skeleton of the building.

The sky courts at the edges of the tower are located next to the structural lift core as pocket parks-in-the-sky. These also serve as interstitial zones between the inside areas and outside areas. Recessed balcony areas with full-height glazed doors open out from the offices. These also serve as emergency evacuation zones as well as areas for planting and landscaping.

Legend
1 Site plan
2 Street level view
3 Sun path diagram
4 Cross-section
5 View from north - east
6 Elevation
7 Elevation

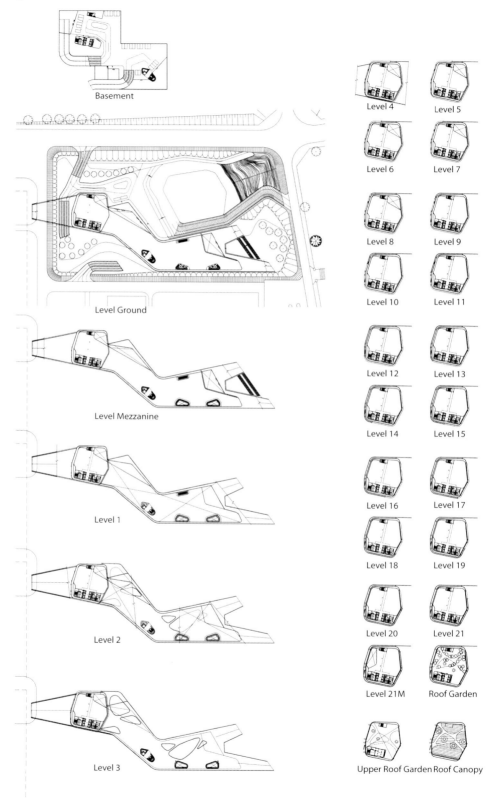

Basement

Level Ground

Level Mezzanine

Level 1

Level 2

Level 3

Level 4

Level 5

Level 6

Level 7

Level 8

Level 9

Level 10

Level 11

Level 12

Level 13

Level 14

Level 15

Level 16

Level 17

Level 18

Level 19

Level 20

Level 21

Level 21M

Roof Garden

Upper Roof Garden

Roof Canopy

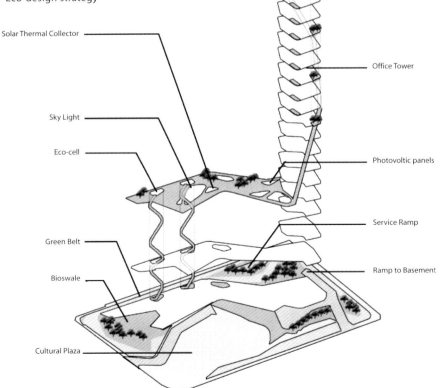

Eco-Cells
The Eco-Cells are vertical cellular voids or slots integrated into the podium. These cellular voids have a spiraling vegetated ramp from the roof garden to the ground and basement levels and bring biomass, vegetation, daylight, rainwater and natural ventilation into its inner depths of the floors.

Vertical Green Belt
This is conceived as part of a linear landscape above the podium, linking the Cultural Plaza from the Ground Plane to the Office Tower. The Vertical Green Belt is planted with different types of trees, shrubs and ground cover plant species to reduce heat island effect, thus reduces the need for the use of renewable energy in air conditioning and cooling.

Legend

Solar Thermal Collector

Sky Light

Eco-cell

Green Belt

Bioswale

Cultural Plaza

Wind Turbine

Continuous Vegetation

Sky Courts

Office Tower

Photovoltaic panels

Service Ramp

Ramp to Basement

Chongqing Tower

11

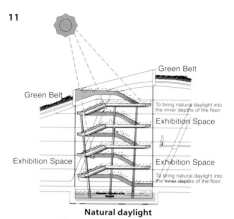

Natural daylight

To bring natural daylight into the inner depths of the floor

Green Belt

Green Belt

Exhibition Space

Exhibition Space

Exhibition Space

To bring natural daylight into the inner depths of the floor

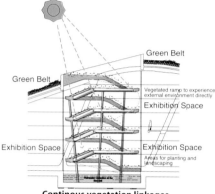

Continous vegetation linkages

Green Belt

Green Belt

Vegetated ramp to experience external environment directly

Exhibition Space

Exhibition Space

Exhibition Space

Areas for planting and landscaping

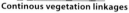

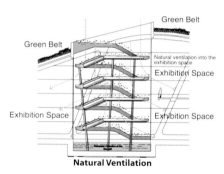

Natural Ventilation

Green Belt

Green Belt

Natural ventilation into the exhibition space

Exhibition Space

Exhibition Space

Exhibition Space

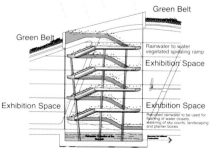

Sewage recycling system

Green Belt

Green Belt

Rainwater to water vegetated spiralling ramp

Exhibition Space

Exhibition Space

Exhibition Space

Recycled rainwater to be used for flushing of water closets, watering of sky courts, landscaping and planter boxes.

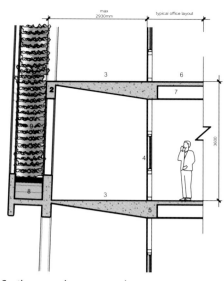

max 2930mm | typical office layout

Continuous and ramp vegetation on external façade

1. Web structure
2. R.C beam on Web structure
3. R.C sun shading
4. External glazing
5. R.C beam
6. R.C slab
7. Ceiling level
8. External vegetated spiralling ramp
9. Steps on vegetated ramp

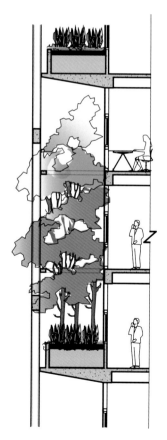

Parks-in-the-sky.

Legend

11 Eco-Cell: Natural daylight
12 Eco-Cell: Continuous vegetation linkage
13 Eco-Cell: Natural ventilation
14 Eco-Cell: Sewerage recycling system
15 Continuous ramp & vegetation
16 Skycourts
17 Eye level view
18 Front view
19 North elevation

Boustead Tower

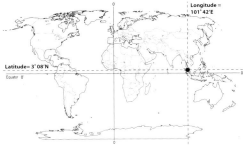

Location
Kuala Lumpur

Climatic Zone
Tropical

Vegetation Zone
Rainforest

No. of Storeys
31

Areas
GFA   : 29,841 sq.m.
NFA   : 22,381 sq.m.

Site Area
208,887 sq.m.

Plot Ratio
1 : 7

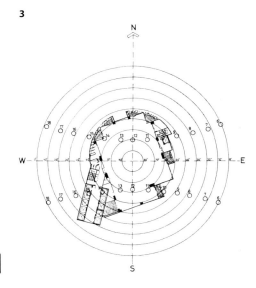

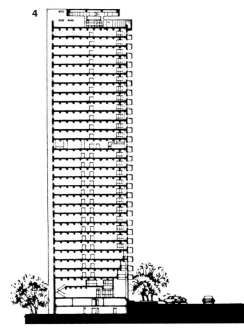

The tower is an early experiment to introduce planted skycourts placed at the corners of all the floors of the builtform. These transitional spaces serve a number of functions; they allow the introduction of planting and landscaping into the upper part of the tower; they provide a flexible zone in which, executive wash rooms or kitchenettes can be added in the future. They provide deep recesses as sun shading to the facade to enable full-height glazing on the hot sides of the tower and in addition the intermediary spaces enhance the quality of natural light. Sliding doors bring natural ventilation into the office work spaces, when required.

The recesses may also be used to conceal supplementary air-conditioning units, if required.

The building's configuration is shaped to respond to the equatorial sun-path. It is clad in a ventilated rain-check aluminum-skin which traps heat and dissipates it before it can be transmitted to the main structure. Lift cores and toilets are located on the hot west and east sides of the builtform as a bioclimatic design principle for towers in the tropical climatic zone. The lift lobby areas receive natural light and ventilation. All the west and east-facing windows are solar protected.

6

7

5

8

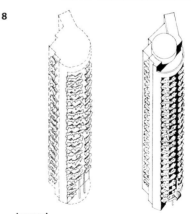

Legend

1 Site plan
2 The planted façade
3 Sun path diagram
4 Cross section
5 View of planting
6 Underside of entrance
7 Planted skycourts
8 Study sketches

9

10

12

11

13

Legend

9   Axonometric view
10 Sun-shaded balcony
11 Irrigation system
12 Full-height ventilation-controlling glazing onto balcony
13 Naturally lit lift lobby
14 General view

1. Uprotected Curtain Wall

Uprotected Glazing

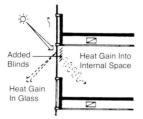

Added Blinds

Heat Gain Into Internal Space

Heat Gain In Glass

3. Recessed Windows

Recessed Windows

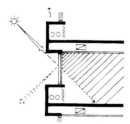

Shaded Area has Reduced Heat Gain

5. Vertical Fins

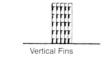

Vertical Fins

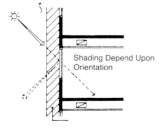

Shading Depend Upon Orientation

2. Deep Recess and Balconies

Recessed Glazing and Balconies

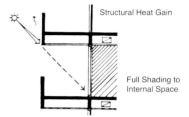

Structural Heat Gain

Full Shading to Internal Space

4. Horizontal Fins

Horizontal Fins

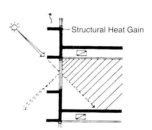

Structural Heat Gain

6. Deep Recess Combined with Balcony Terraces, Planters, Heat-Sink Cladding

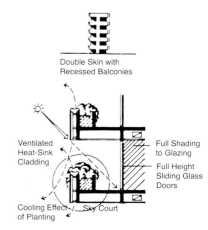

Double Skin with Recessed Balconies

Ventilated Heat-Sink Cladding

Full Shading to Glazing

Full Height Sliding Glass Doors

Cooling Effect of Planting

Sky Court

16

Cladding —

Terrace

Masonary

Ventilating Zone

17

Boustead Tower

18

19

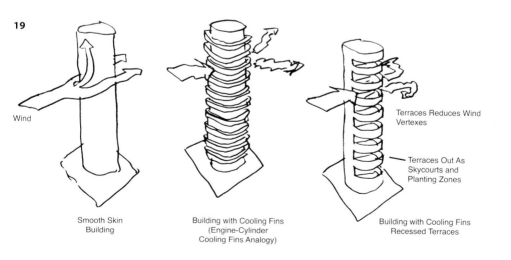

Wind

Terraces Reduces Wind
Vertexes

Terraces Out As
Skycourts and
Planting Zones

Smooth Skin
Building

Building with Cooling Fins
(Engine-Cylinder
Cooling Fins Analogy)

Building with Cooling Fins
Recessed Terraces

Legend

15 Principles and detail of the development of low-energy shading

16 Cladding detail showing ventilation zone

17 General view

18 Planting

19 Wind-study sketches

Palomas 2 Tower

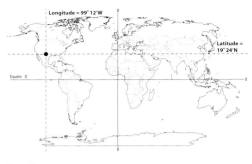

Location
Mexico City

Climatic Zone
Dry

Vegetation Zone
Desert-scrub

No. of Storeys
16

Areas
GFA   : 7,087 sq.m.
NFA   : 5,112 sq.m.

Site Area
735 sq.m.

Plot Ratio
1 : 9.6

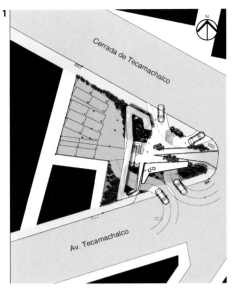

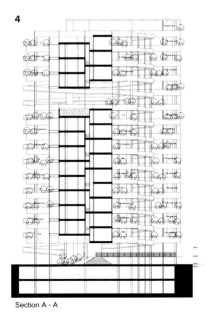

Section A - A

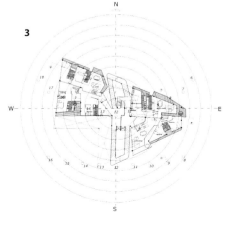

The apartment tower is located on an urban corner plot in an upmarket neighbourhood. The site's terrain and the surrounding streets slope, with a difference of around five metres between the highest and lowest part of the site.

The typical floor has four units of split-level apartments. The apartments are placed at the ends of the tower, while the centre is allocated to the elevator core and stairs.

This central area is open and naturally lit and ventilated. All the apartments can be naturally ventilated.

An evaporative cooling shaft draws fresh air from the top of the tower and ventilates the central zone of the tower.

A communal sky garden for residents is provided midway up the tower, as a recreational space and as a viewing platform where the best views of the landscape to the south can be enjoyed.

To maximize the enjoyment of the views, the apartments are configured as cross-over split level units, so that every unit has a view to the south. This cross-over arrangement is reflected externally and this together with the vegetated private balconies and sky gardens characterises the aesthetic of the building.

5

Palomas 2 Tower

Legend
1 Site plan
2 General view
3 Sun path diagram
4 Cross-section
5 Vertical landscaping

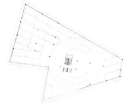

Basement 02 Plan

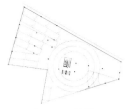

Basement 01 Plan

Av. Tecamachalco

Level 01 Plan

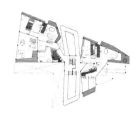

Level 02 Plan

Level 03 Plan

Level 04 Plan

Level 05 Plan

Level 06 Plan

Level 07 Plan

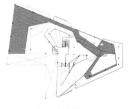

Level 11 Plan

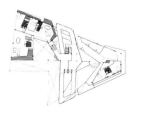

Level 12 Plan

7

Legend

6 Summary of plans
7 Conceptual / environmental section

Al-Ghorfa Tower

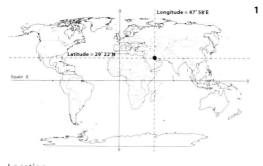

1

Location
Kuwait

Climatic Zone
Dry

Vegetation Zone
Desert-scrub

No. of Storeys
40

Areas
GFA　　　: 16,400 sq.m.
NFA　　　: 28,938 sq.m.

Site Area
1,500 sq.m.

Plot Ratio
1 : 9.2

2

4

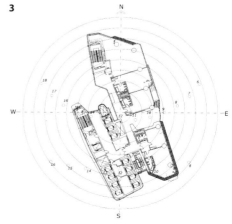

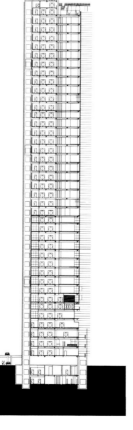

3

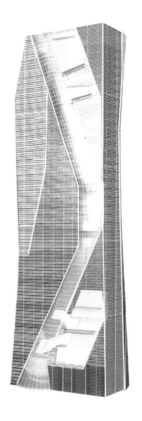

The tower is a multi-use structure that comprises offices, retail, restaurants, banquet halls, business centre and conference rooms, a swimming pool, nine hotel floors, a multi-purpose hall and a helipad.

The tower is configured in two distinctively shaped, yet connected vertical parts forming one single tower incorporating 'served' and 'serviced' components. The serviced areas of the tower are orientated to optimise on the water front views.

The key feature is a weaving large atrium that ascends up the north façade of the tower. Traditional courtyards are re-interpreted here as courtyards-in-the-sky.

The tower is crafted to bioclimatically respond with passive mode strategies related to the hot-arid climatic conditions of the locality and with a mixed mode atrium at the façade.

The atrium includes an evaporative cooling zone and the sky courts also serve as informal meeting spaces and viewing platforms. The intermediate vegetated sky courts and the water features create milder microclimate conditions at the edges of the office floors. Lift lobbies have natural daylight and are also designed as secondary meeting places.

The layered façade as a passive mode feature reduces the air conditioning load. The narrow-plan enables the internal areas of the floor plates to be accessible by daylight, reducing dependency on artificial lighting. External louvres control solar insolation and protect against sand storms. The north atrium creates a cool microclimate zone to this façade.

5

6

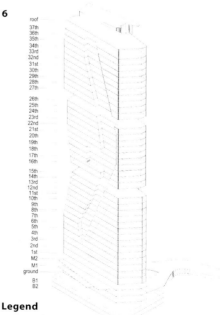

roof
37th
36th
35th
34th
33rd
32nd
31st
30th
29th
28th
27th
26th
25th
24th
23rd
22nd
21st
20th
19th
18th
17th
16th
15th
14th
13rd
12nd
11st
10th
9th
8th
7th
6th
5th
4th
3rd
2nd
1st
M2
M1
ground
B1
B2

7

Legend
1 Site plan
2 North view
3 Sun path diagram
4 Cross-section
5 View from south east
6 Wireframe of the tower
7 Podium atrium

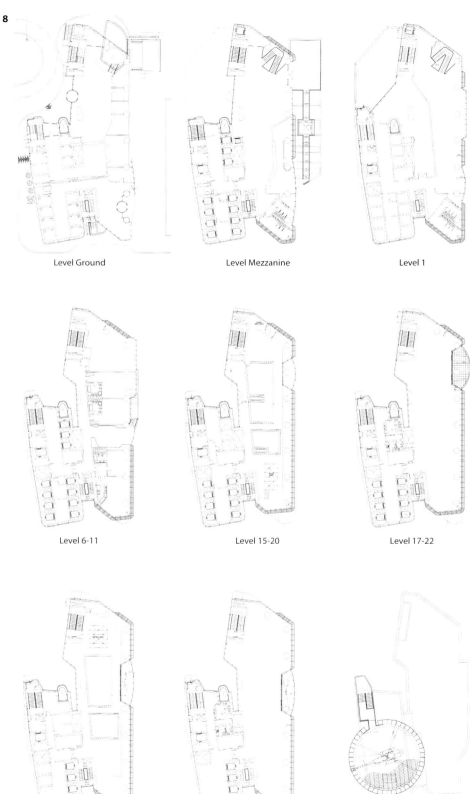

Level Ground

Level Mezzanine

Level 1

Level 6-11

Level 15-20

Level 17-22

Level 27-32

Level 29-34

Level Roof

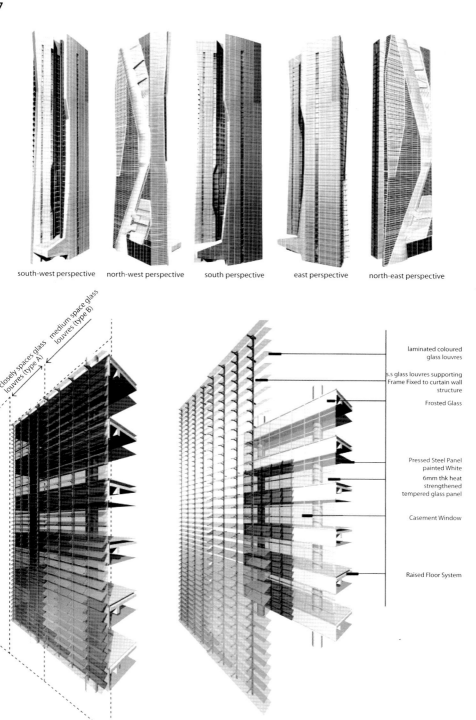

south-west perspective north-west perspective south perspective east perspective north-east perspective

closely spaces glass louvres (type A)

medium space glass louvres (type B)

laminated coloured glass louvres

s.s glass louvres supporting Frame Fixed to curtain wall structure

Frosted Glass

Pressed Steel Panel painted White

6mm thk heat strengthened tempered glass panel

Casement Window

Raised Floor System

Al-Ghorfa Tower

Curtain Wall Facade with External Glass Louvres of different spacing

Facade System of Curtain Wall with External Glass Louvres

Legend

8 Summary of plans
9 Elevations
10 Façade system

Beijing World Science & Trade Centre

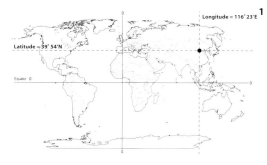

Location
Beijing

Climatic Zone
Cold

Vegetation Zone
Deciduous Forest

No. of Storeys
Apartment towers	: 50, 62 & 72
Office tower	: 43
Hotel & Convention Centre	: 25
Service Apartment	: 11

Areas
| GFA | : 173,582 sq.m. |
| NFA | : 130,187 sq.m. |

Site Area
92,100

Plot Ratio
1 : 5.5

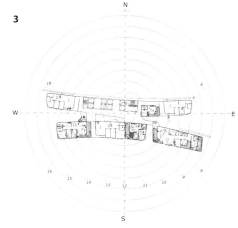

This large urban structure spans across a number of city-blocks and is essentially a podium with a central multiuse cultural plaza, surrounded by a number of office and apartment towers on its east and west frontages.

The dominant ecological feature of the design is a linear green park which extends from the western corner of the site, at street level, and connects to all parts of the built form via landscaped ramps and bridges. The greenery extends into the lower levels of the office towers, which also contain a variety of garden skycourts.

The apartments have good day lighting, views and cross-ventilation opportunities. Each apartment has a garden terrace with a secondary layer of adjustable glass shutters that enclose the spaces in winter acting as a green house, while in summer they are opened to encourage natural cooling.

The paired gateway office towers have a split-plan with an atria. Large moveable vertical screen-blades modify the internal environment by deflecting or scooping wind into the atrium space. Essentially, the complexity of the programme and the ecological responses are exemplified by using the podium as a subscraper and a collector of cultural and commercial activities, leaving the towers to define the skyline.

Legend
1 Site plan
2 Section
3 Sun path diagram
4 Section B-B
5 Night view from the west
6 View from East 3rd Ring Road
7 View from the park bridge and pedestrian way
8 The cultural plaza

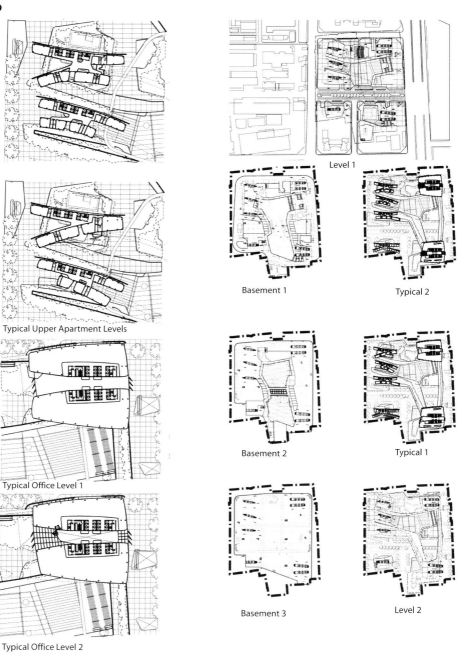

Typical Upper Apartment Levels

Typical Office Level 1

Typical Office Level 2

Level 1

Basement 1

Typical 2

Basement 2

Typical 1

Basement 3

Level 2

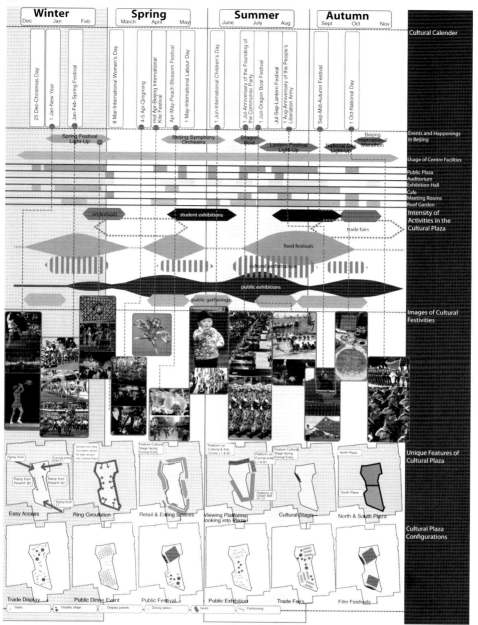

The chart is titled with a running vertical label on the right side: "Beijing World Science & Trade Centre"

Seasons across the top:

Winter			Spring			Summer			Autumn		
Dec	Jan	Feb	March	April	May	June	July	Aug	Sept	Oct	Nov

Row labels on the right side of the chart:
- Cultural Calender
- Events and Happenings in Beijing
- Usage of Centre Facilties
- Public Plaza
- Auditorium
- Exhibition Hall
- Cafe
- Meeting Rooms
- Roof Garden
- Intensity of Activities in the Cultural Plaza
- Images of Cultural Festivities
- Unique Features of Cultural Plaza
- Cultural Plaza Configurations

Cultural Calendar entries:
25 Dec-Christmas Day; 1 Jan-New Year; Jan-Feb-Spring Festival; 8 Mar-International Women's Day; 4-5 Apr-Qingming; mid Apr-Beijing International Kite Festival; Apr-May-Peach Blossom Festival; 1 May-International Labour Day; 1 Jun-International Children's Day; 1 Jul-Anniversary of the Founding of the Communist Party; 1 Jun-Dragon Boat Festival; Jul-Sep-Lantern Festival; 1 Aug-Anniversary of the People's Liberation Army; Sep-Mid-Autumn Festival; 1 Oct-National Day

Events and Happenings in Beijing:
Spring Festival Light-Up; Beijing Symphony Orchestra; Dragon Boat; Lantern Festival Light-Up; National Day Light-Up; Beijing International Marathon

Intensity of Activities in the Cultural Plaza:
art festivals; student exhibitions; trade fairs; food festivals; cultural performances; public exhibitions; public gatherings

Unique Features of Cultural Plaza (with plan diagrams):
Access from Ring Circulation allows for easy access into Cultural Plaza; Ramp from L1; Formal entry from L1; Ramp from Retail@ B2; Ramp from Retail@ B2; Ramp from L1; Feature Cultural Stage facing Formal Entry; Platform on Cultural & Arts Centre L1 & B1; Platform on Formal entry L1 & B1; Platform on Green Belt on L2; Feature Cultural Stage facing Formal Entry; North Plaza; South Plaza

Labels under plans: Easy Access; Ring Circulation; Retail & Eating Spaces; Viewing Platforms looking into Plaza; Cultural Stage; North & South Plaza

Cultural Plaza Configurations labels:
Trade Display; Public Dining Event; Public Festival; Public Exhibition; Trade Fairs; Film Festivals

Legend at bottom: Stalls; Display stage; Display panels; Dining tables; Seats; Partitioning

Legend
9 Summary of plans
10 Bioclimatic responses chart

Business Advancement Technology Centre (BATC)

Longitude = 13° 24'W
Latitude = 52° 31'N
Equator 0

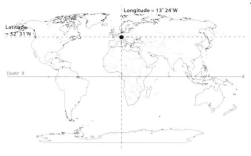

Location
Germany

Climatic Zone
Cold

Vegetation Zone
Alpine

No. of Storeys
60

Areas
GFA   : 708,178 sq.m.
NFA   : 530,669 sq.m.

Site Area
167,286 sq.m.

Plot Ratio
1 : 4

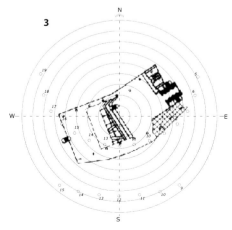

The cluster of towers including a principal signature tower is located in a 47-acre landscaped park where the group of buildings is served by a number of public plazas, tree-lined walkways, car access routes and two landscaped bridges that ecologically traverse the site. The public Light Rail Transit System (LRT) is integrated into the form with its central station placed at the junction between the retail and commercial facilities and the university.

The buildings are placed within a landscaped ground plane. Water gardens and soft landscaping define the pedestrian routes throughout the site. All areas within the site are linked by a semi-enclosed pedestrian network located at the lower plaza level, providing semi-protected car-free access to the various components within the site.

Landscaped terraces and sky courts are incorporated in all floors of the office towers providing building occupants with the opportunity to access green surroundings.

To maintain visual and ecological connectivity between floors, these sky courts form a continuous vertical link, both visually and physically.

5

6

7

9

8

Legend
1 Site plan
2 Signature tower
3 Sun path diagram
4 Elevation
5 Elevation showing vegetation
6 Aerial view
7 3D Aerial view
8 Elevation
9 Elevation

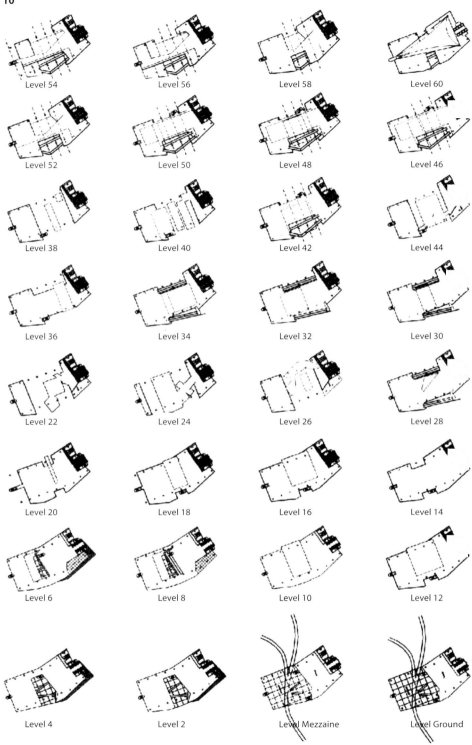

Level 54   Level 56   Level 58   Level 60

Level 52   Level 50   Level 48   Level 46

Level 38   Level 40   Level 42   Level 44

Level 36   Level 34   Level 32   Level 30

Level 22   Level 24   Level 26   Level 28

Level 20   Level 18   Level 16   Level 14

Level 6   Level 8   Level 10   Level 12

Level 4   Level 2   Level Mezzaine   Level Ground

11

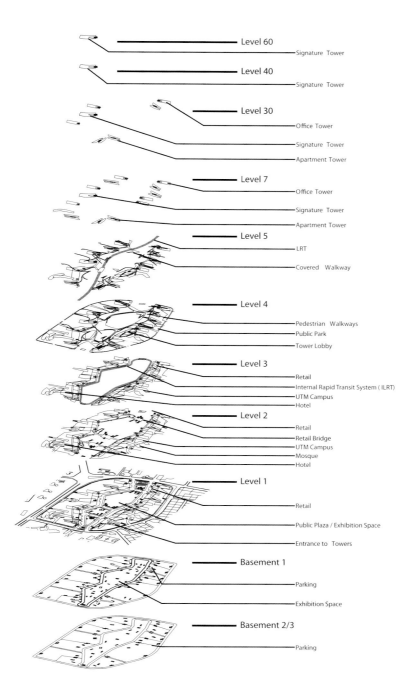

Level 60
Signature Tower

Level 40
Signature Tower

Level 30
Office Tower
Signature Tower
Apartment Tower

Level 7
Office Tower
Signature Tower
Apartment Tower

Level 5
LRT
Covered Walkway

Level 4
Pedestrian Walkways
Public Park
Tower Lobby

Level 3
Retail
Internal Rapid Transit System (ILRT)
UTM Campus
Hotel

Level 2
Retail
Retail Bridge
UTM Campus
Mosque
Hotel

Level 1
Retail
Public Plaza / Exhibition Space
Entrance to Towers

Basement 1
Parking
Exhibition Space

Basement 2/3
Parking

12

Legend
10 Summary of plans
11 Axonometric floor plans diagram
12 Aerial view of BATC development

13

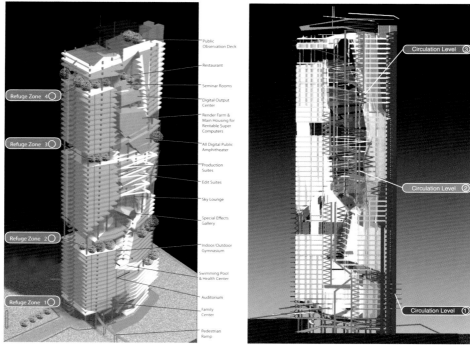

14

15

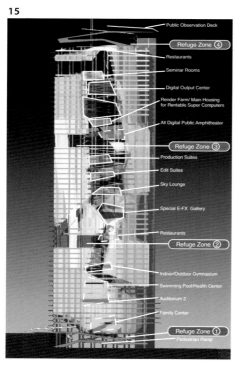

16

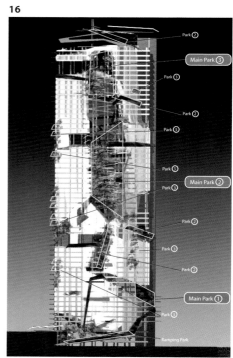

17

18

19

Legend

Elephant & Castle Towers

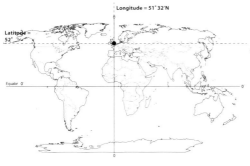

Longitude = 51°32'N

Latitude = 52°

Equator 0

Location
London

Climatic Zone
Temperate

Vegetation Zone
Deciduous

No. of Storeys
35/12

Areas
GFA   : 372,069 sq.m.
NFA   : 311,580 sq.m.

Site Area
687,973 sq.m.

Plot Ratio
1:3/1:7

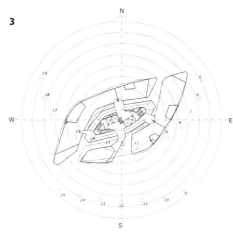

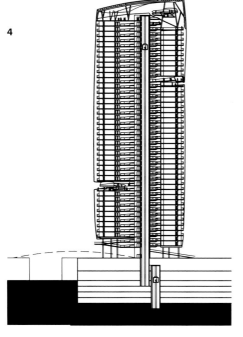

The project consists of three towers for residential use, placed above a retail and commercial podium area adjoining the train station.

The lifts and staircores are brought together in a compact central configuration encircled by a ventilated and landscaped internal passageway ramp.

The typical oval shaped floor has a two-sided arrangement, which offers a variety of unit - orientation and views. Inserted into the built form are a number of 'sky-pod' volumes for communal uses and the summit of the towers has a large winter garden, which outwardly signals the building's ecological presence incorporated into its built form.

Landscaping is incorporated within the private gardens to the dwelling units and the communal sky-parks within the towers give users a humane habitable green environment. In summer, the vertical landscaping absorbs and reflects a high percentage of solar radiation thereby reducing ambient temperatures. The surfaces of the grassed terraces also contribute to a cooler and healthier building.

The eco-tower is also configured to indicate a visible elevated social - openness.

5
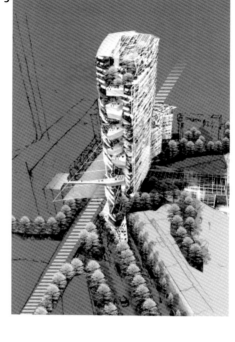

6
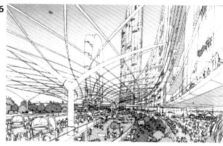

8

7

Legend
1 Site plan
2 Aerial view of the tower and site context
3 Sun path diagram
4 Cross-section
5 Aerial view
6 Street view
7 View from apartment
8 Green linkages

9

Level 1	Level 2	Level 3	Level 4	Level 5
Level 6	Level 7	Level 8	Level 9	Level 10
Level 11	Level 12	Level 13	Level 14	Level 15
Level 16	Level 17	Level 18	Level 19	Level 20
Level 21	Level 22	Level 23	Level 24	Level 25
Level 26	Level 27	Level 28	Level 29	Level 30
Level 31	Level 32	Level 33	Level 34	Level 35
Level 36	Level 37	Level 38	Level 39	Level 40

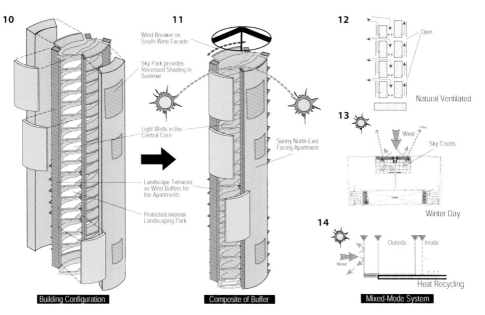

10

Wind Breaker on South-West Facade

Sky Park provides Recessed Shading in Summer

Light Wells in the Central Core

Landscape Terraces as Wind Buffers for the Apartments

Protected Internal Landscaping Park

Building Configuration

11

Sunny North-East Facing Apartment

Composite of Buffer

12

Open

Natural Ventilated

13

Wind

Sky Courts

Winter Day

14

Outside | Inside

Wind

Heat Recycling

Mixed-Mode System

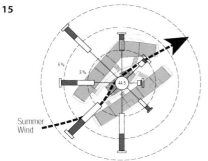

15

Summer Wind

6 %

3 %

44.5

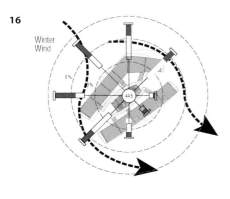

16

Winter Wind

6 %

44.5

17

18

Legend

 9 Summary of plans
10 Building configuration
11 Composite of buffer
12 Natural ventilation
13 Winter day
14 Mixed-mode system
15 Summer windrose
16 Winter windrose
17 Elevation
18 Elevation

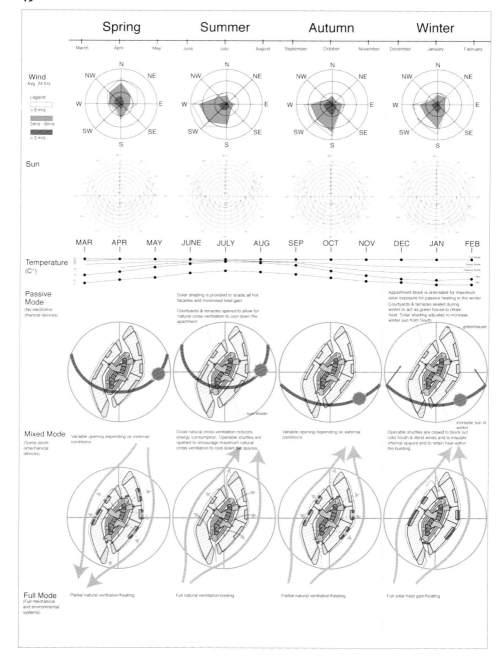

	Spring	Summer	Autumn	Winter
	March April May	June July August	September October November	December January February

Wind
Avg. 24 hrs

Legend
> 6 m/s
3m/s - 6m/s
< 3 m/s

Sun

MAR APR MAY JUNE JULY AUG SEP OCT NOV DEC JAN FEB

Temperature
(C°)

Mode
Mixed Mode
Passive Mode
Max
Min

Passive Mode
(No electromechanical devices)

Solar shading is provided to shade all hot facades and minimised heat gain

Courtyards & terraces opened to allow for natural cross ventilation to cool down the apartment

Appartment block is orientated for maximum solar exposure for passive heating in the winter

Courtyards & terraces sealed during winter to act as green house to retain heat. Solar shading adjusted to increase winter sun from South

greenhouse

sun shade

increase sun in winter

Mixed Mode
(Some electromechanical devices)

Variable opening depending on external conditions

Good natural cross-ventilation reduces energy consumption. Operable shutters are opened to encourage maximum natural cross-ventilation to cool down the spaces

Variable opening depending on external conditions

Operable shutters are closed to block out cold South & West winds and to insulate internal spaces and to retain heat within the building

Full Mode
(Full mechanical and environmental systems)

Partial natural ventilation/heating

Full natural ventilation/cooling

Partial natural ventilation/heating

Full solar heat gain/heating

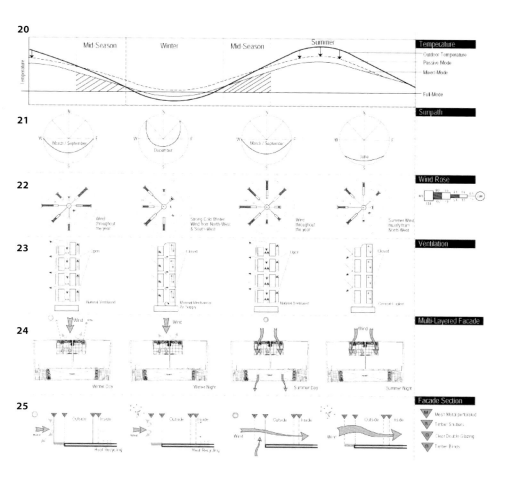

20

Temperature
- Outdoor Temperature
- Passive Mode
- Mixed Mode
- Full Mode

Mid-Season · Winter · Mid-Season · Summer

21

Sunpath

March / September · December · March / September · June

22

Wind Rose

Wind throughout the year · Strong Cold Winter Wind from North-West & South-West · Wind throughout the year · Summer Wind mostly from North-West

23

Ventilation

Open · Closed · Open · Closed

Natural Ventilated · Minimal Mechanical Air Supply · Natural Ventilated · Constant Cooled

24

Multi-Layered Facade

Wind · Wind · Wind

Winter Day · Winter Night · Summer Day · Summer Night

25

Facade Section
- Mesh Metal perforated
- Timber Shutters
- Clear Double Glazing
- Timber Blinds

Outside · Inside · Outside · Inside · Outside · Inside · Outside · Inside

Heat Recycling · Heat Recycling

26

Legend

19 Composite bioclimatic response chart
20 Temperature
21 Sun path
22 Wind rose
23 Ventilation options
24 Multi-layered façade
26 Elevation

Ho Chi Minh City Tower

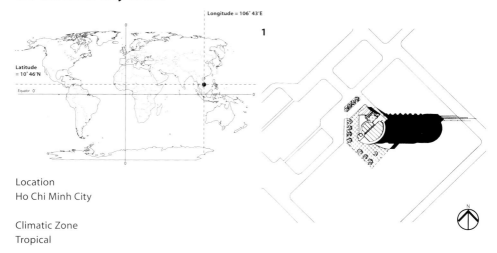

Location
Ho Chi Minh City

Climatic Zone
Tropical

Vegetation Zone
Rainforest

No. of Storeys
26

Areas
GFA   : 14,286 sq.m.
NFA   : 19,684 sq.m.

Site Area
148,574 sq.m.

Plot Ratio
1:10.4

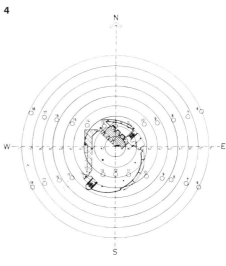

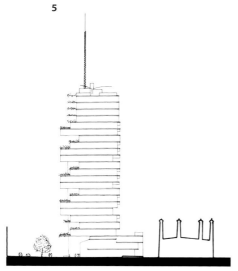

78

The principal concept for the tower is as a 'boulevard in the sky'. The tower is located at the end of a boulevard in this French-influenced former colonial city with the tower emulating its horizontal tree-lined avenues as a vertical extension through a series of sky courts, planted trellises that surround the glass lifts, and a roof-top planted penthouse.

The lift lobbies, stairways and toilets have naturally ventilated opportunities and are daylit as low-energy spaces.

Bridges off the lift lobbies give access to the sky courts.

The west side of the building has sliding glass-doors that control the extent of natural ventilation entering the office spaces (when required or when regular air - conditioning is switched off during the frequent brown-outs in the city).

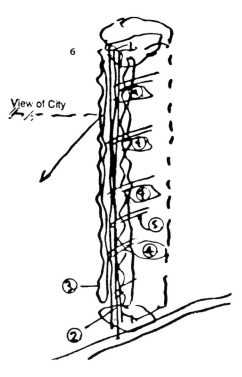

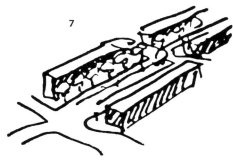

Legend
1 Site plan
2 The city boulevard showing tree-lined sides, squares, intersections and begining and end focal points
3 Urban context model
4 Sun path diagram
5 Cross-section
6 The boulevard in the sky
7 Sketch of the city boulevard
8 Bird's-eye view of model
9 View of model from north-west

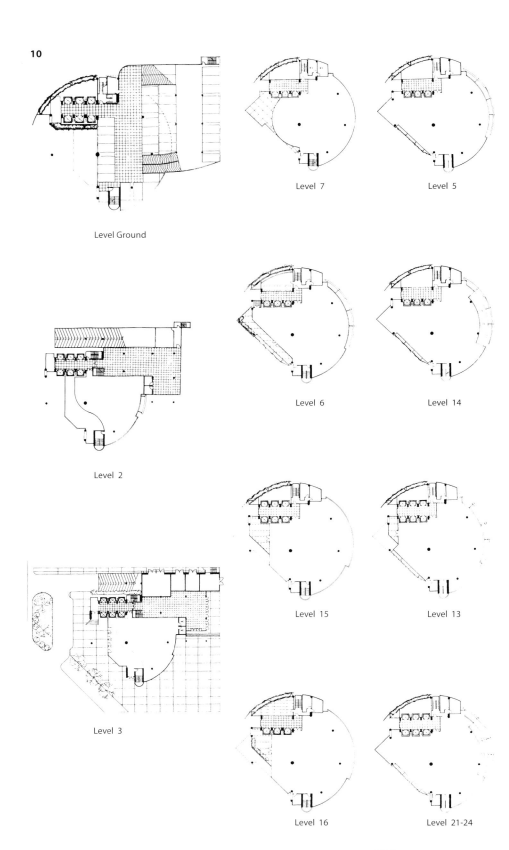

10

Level Ground

Level 7

Level 5

Level 2

Level 6

Level 14

Level 3

Level 15

Level 13

Level 16

Level 21-24

Summary of Plans

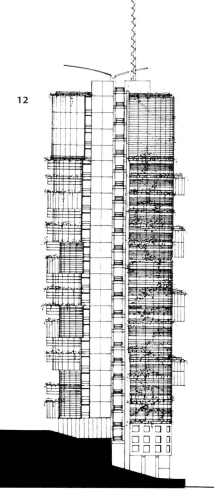

Legend

10 Summary of plans
11 View from west
12 Elevation
13 Model showing sky court and penthouse
14 View of the entrance

IBM Plaza

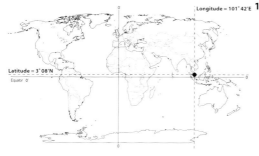

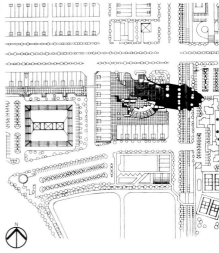

Location
Kuala Lumpur

Climatic Zone
Tropical

Vegetation Zone
Rainforest

No. of Storeys
24

Areas
GFA   : 26,047 sq.m.
NFA   : 17,496 sq.m.

Site Area
80,939 sq.m.

Plot Ratio
1 : 3

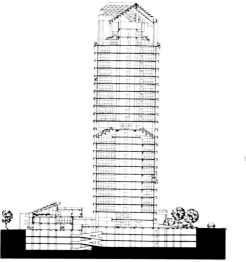

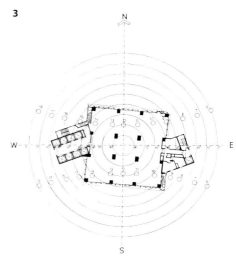

The office tower is linked by a curvilinear bridge to a lower two-storey restaurant / food court block juxtaposed within a plaza. The surrounding roads are pedestrianised and connect to adjoining shophouses.

Two geometries are bioclimatically acknowledged in the built form that of the sun's path and that of the context. Typical floors are aligned north - south relating to the path of the sun. The elevator core and escape stairs are on the east and west (being the hot) sides in this equatorial location. The configuration of the built form is in a direct response to the local tropical climate.

The top of the tower is pitched – an evocative cultural reminder of the traditional house form. Local plants are introduced in a vertical stepped system of planter-boxes combined with trellises which start from a landscaped mound at the ground level and rise diagonally up the face of the building. At mid-level, these planters traverse horizontally across the breeze-way and are stepped up again diagonally on the other face of the building to the roof terraces.

The ground floor entrance lift lobby leading to the plaza is open to the outside space and is naturally ventilated. The upper floors extend in an asymmetrical pattern resulting in wedge-shaped projections and an overall built form which is irregular as a deviation from the regular slab form of conventional towers.

5

6

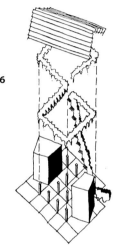

I B M P l a z a

8

7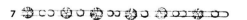

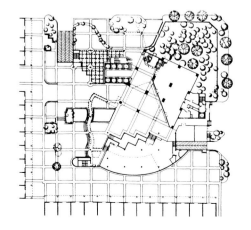

Legend
1 Site plan
2 General view
3 Sun path diagram
4 Cross-section
5 Ground floor plaza
6 Vertical landscaping concept
7 Ground floor plan
8 Balconies and planters cutting across the facade of the building

9

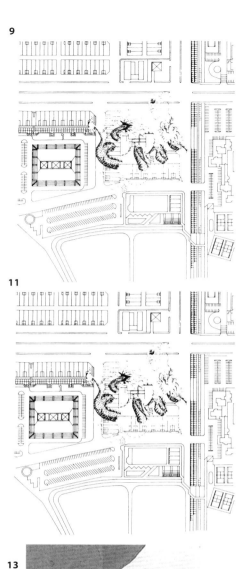

10

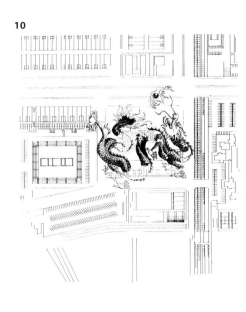

11

12

13

14

15

I
B
M

P
l
a
z
a

Legend

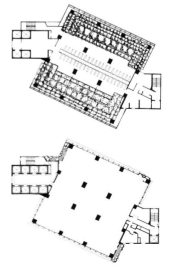

20

21

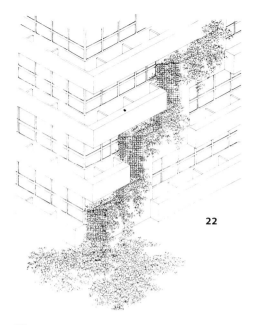

22

24

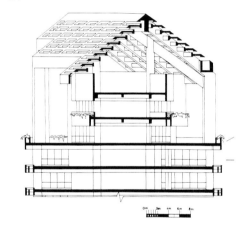

23

Legend
16 Planted balconies
17 Shading provided by deep recesses
18 Typical floor plan
19 Mid-Level planted floor plan
20 Street level view
21 Detail of bridge
22 View of plaza
23 Planter detail
24 Detail showing filter roof

National Library Building

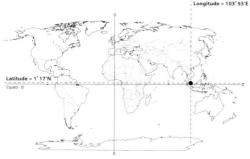

Location
Singapore

Climatic Zone
Tropical

Vegetation Zone
Rainforest

No. of Storeys
16

Areas
GFA   : 58,783 sq.m.
NFA   : 44,087 sq.m.

Site Area
11,304 sq.m.

Plot Ratio
1 : 5.2

1

2

4

3

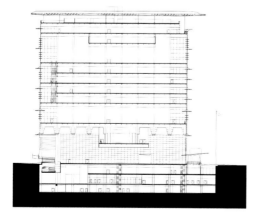

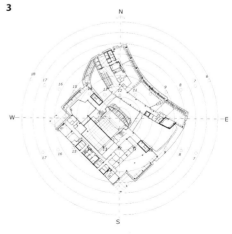

The building is a state-of-the-art high-rise library that consists of two interlinked blocks separated by a day-lit-semi-enclosed internal 'street' with a louvered roof canopy.

The two-blocks are connected by bridges at their upper levels. The pedestrian 'street' below retains the existent visual axis from the southern street to a church to the north of the site.

The larger regular shaped block houses the various library collections and straddles over an open-to-the-sky naturally ventilated civic plaza that is designed to enable semi enclosed 'outdoor' cultural events to be held as well as alfresco-style cafes.

The library is designed as a low energy environment responsive structure. Passive mode design strategies to enable this to be a high-comfort building include appropriate built form orientation in relation to the sun path, good daylight optimisation, solar orientation, sunshading, light-shelves, natural ventilation to interstitial spaces, responsive façade design, use of appropriate building colours (white) and the use of extensive landscaping at the ground plane and at a number of skycourts at the façades.

The central atrium creates a cool microclimate zone while allowing natural daylight to reach the circulation areas within the building.

Wide sunshades control direct sunlight and glare besides creating the aesthetic of a contemporary climatic-responsive built-form. The elevator service - cores serve as thermal buffers to the hot north - west and the south - west façades reducing heat gain. The garden skycourts provide a green, visually relaxing environment for the library users while enhancing the site's biodiversity.

Legend
1 Site plan
2 Day view
3 Sun path diagram
4 Cross-section
5 Lobby
6 External sunshade façade
7 Landscaping
8 Night view

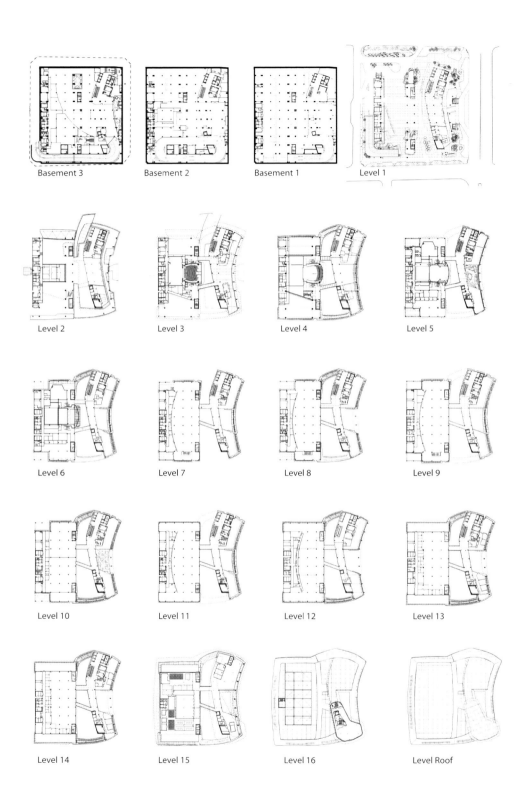

Basement 3

Basement 2

Basement 1

Level 1

Level 2

Level 3

Level 4

Level 5

Level 6

Level 7

Level 8

Level 9

Level 10

Level 11

Level 12

Level 13

Level 14

Level 15

Level 16

Level Roof

9

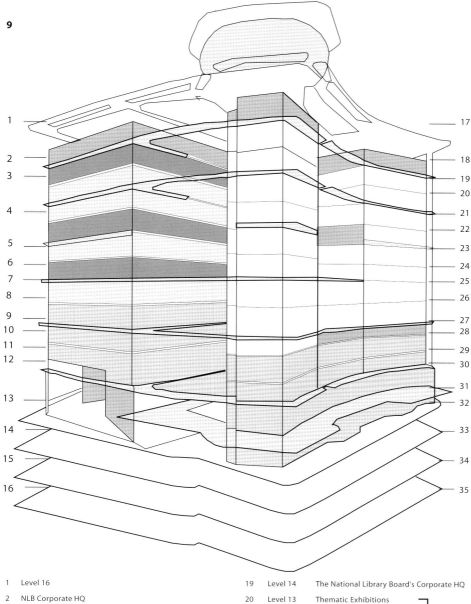

1   Level 16

2   NLB Corporate HQ

3   Rare Collections

4   Singapore & Southeast Asia Collections

5   Asian Children's & Donor's Collections

6   Chinese, Malay & Tamil Collections

7   Art & Business Collections

8   Social Science & Humanities Collections Science
    & Technology Collections

9   Drama Centre

10 Drama Centre

11 Drama Centre

12 Drama Centre (500 pax seatings)

13 Plaza & Lobby

14 Central Lending Library

15 Central Lending Library

16 Central Lending Library

17 Level 16   Observatory Pod

18 Level 15   M & E Plant

19 Level 14   The National Library Board's Corporate HQ

20 Level 13   Thematic Exhibitions

21 Level 12   Thematic Exhibitions

22 Level 11   Permanent Exhibitions

23 Level 10   Thematic Exhibitions, Skycourt

24 Level 9   Thematic Exhibitions

25 Level 8   Thematic Exhibitions

26 Level 7   Thematic Exhibitions

Lee Kong
Chian
Reference
Library

27 Level 6   Drama Centre, Permanent
28 Level 5   Exhibitions, Skycourt

29 Level 4   Drama Centre

30 Level 3   Drama Centre

31 Level 2
32 Level 1   Plaza and Lobby

33 Basement 1   Main Collection and Eco-cells

34 Basement 2   Carpark

35 Basement 3   Carpark

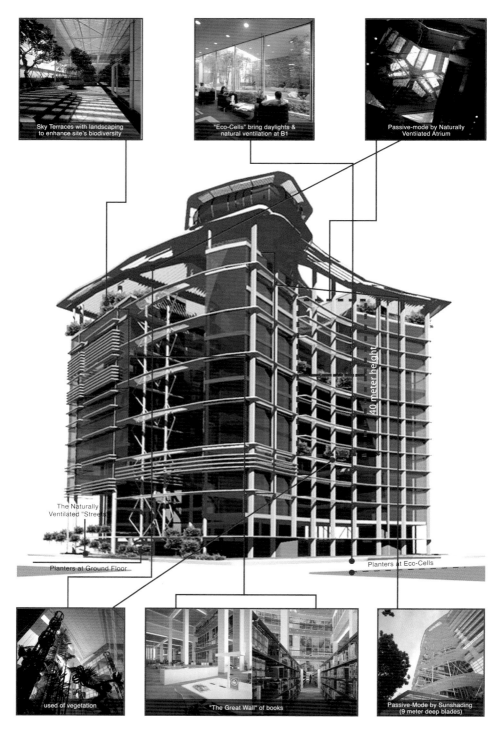

Sky Terraces with landscaping to enhance site's biodiversity

"Eco-Cells" bring daylights & natural ventilation at B1

Passive-mode by Naturally Ventilated Atrium

40 meter height

The Naturally Ventilated "Streets"

Planters at Ground Floor

Planters at Eco-Cells

used of vegetation

"The Great Wall" of books

Passive-Mode by Sunshading (9 meter deep blades)

Passive-mode Low-energy Design Strategies

Legend

8　Summary of plans
9　Library's programme
10　Green features diagram

11

12

13

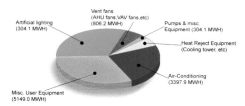

Artificial lighting
(304.1 MWH)

Vent fans
(AHU fans,VAV fans,etc)
(806.2 MWH)

Pumps & misc.
Equipment (304.1 MWH)

Heat Reject Equipment
(Cooling tower, etc)

Air-Conditioning
(3397.9 MWH)

Misc. User Equipment
(5149.0 MWH)

14

15

16

Legend

11 Observation tower
12 Corridor overlooking green atrium
13 Energy pie
14 The street
15 Atrium
16 View from north bridge road

Shanghai Armoury Tower

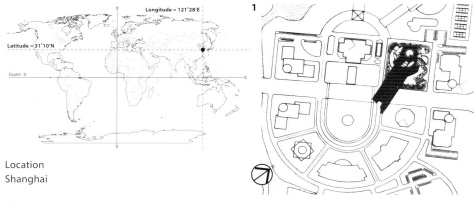

Location
Shanghai

Climatic Zone
Temperate

Vegetation Zone
Rainforest

No. of Storeys
36

Areas
GFA   : 46,750 sq.m.
NFA   : 35,663 sq.m.

Site Area
9,100 sq.m.

Plot Ratio
1 : 5.1

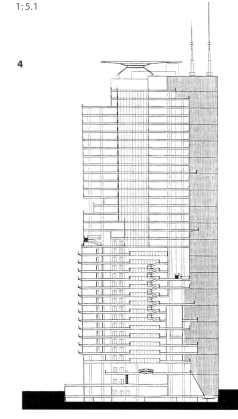

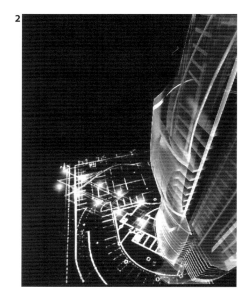

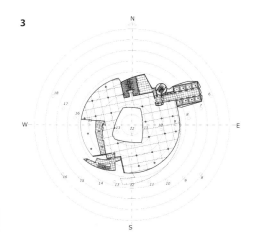

This tower is a symbolic interpretation of components found in military armaments. The sweeping panels of metallic screens on the exterior façade act as solar shields and allude to the armour of the Chinese warrior. The external and internal design features adopt a bioclimatic approach to produce an operationally energy-efficient building that makes the most of the coastal climatic conditions of the locality and allows the occupants to experience the changing seasons of the year.

Landscaped skyterraces are placed at strategic points in the tower as buffer zones between the inside and the outside. In addition they act as oxygen generating 'green lungs', which refresh the microclimate of the periphery of the building. The external weather-screen performs as a multi-functional filter against extreme climatic conditions while allowing panoramic views of the surrounding urban - space.The blending of bioclimatic devices into the architecture of the tower produces a building unique in design and style and is an iconic symbol for the owners.

5

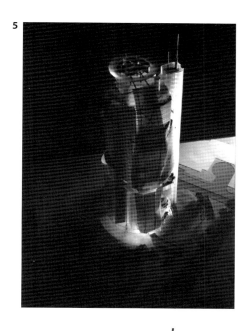

6

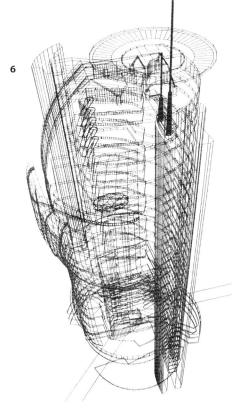

Shanghai Armoury Tower

Legend
1 Site plan
2 Aerial view from south - east
3 Sun path diagram
4 Cross-section
5 View from north - east
6 Wireframe of the tower

7

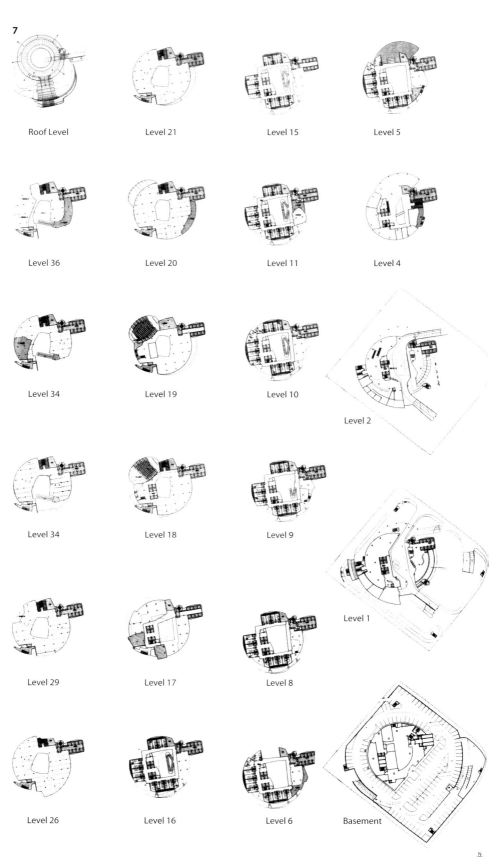

Roof Level

Level 21

Level 15

Level 5

Level 36

Level 20

Level 11

Level 4

Level 34

Level 19

Level 10

Level 2

Level 34

Level 18

Level 9

Level 1

Level 29

Level 17

Level 8

Level 26

Level 16

Level 6

Basement

8

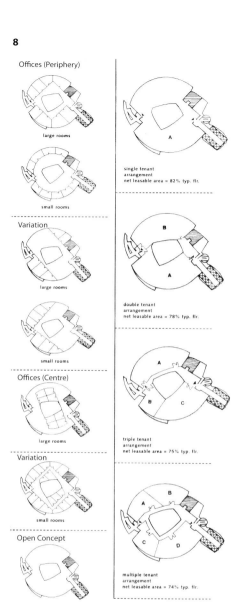

Offices (Periphery)

large rooms

small rooms

single tenant
arrangement
net leasable area = 82% typ. flr.

Variation

large rooms

small rooms

double tenant
arrangement
net leasable area = 78% typ. flr.

Offices (Centre)

large rooms

triple tenant
arrangement
net leasable area = 75% typ. flr.

Variation

small rooms

Open Concept

multiple tenant
arrangement
net leasable area = 74% typ. flr.

9

10

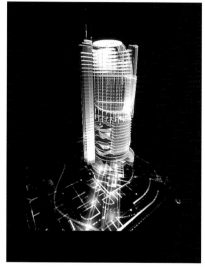

Shanghai Armoury Tower

11

Legend
7 Summary of plans
8 Diagrams
9 North-west view
10 North view
11 West elevation

12

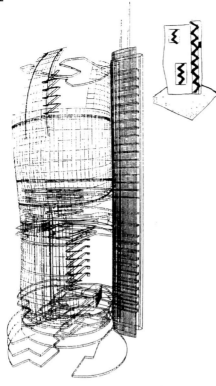

Vertical Circulation

13

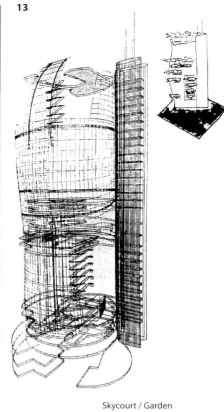

Skycourt / Garden

14

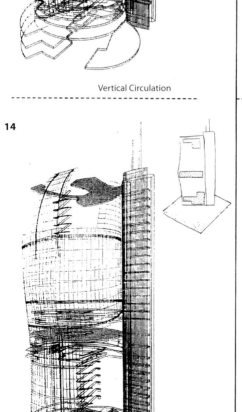

Public Space / Realm

15

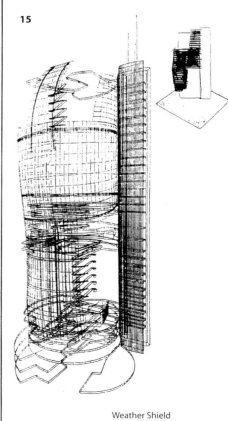

Weather Shield

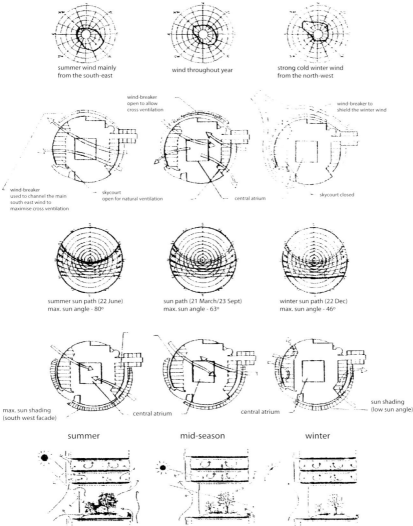

summer wind mainly
from the south-east

wind throughout year

strong cold winter wind
from the north-west

wind-breaker
open to allow
cross ventilation

wind-breaker to
shield the winter wind

wind-breaker
used to channel the main
south east wind to
maximise cross ventilation

skycourt
open for natural ventilation

central atrium

skycourt closed

summer sun path (22 June)
max. sun angle - 80°

sun path (21 March/23 Sept)
max. sun angle - 63°

winter sun path (22 Dec)
max. sun angle - 46°

max. sun shading
(south west facade)

central atrium

central atrium

sun shading
(low sun angle)

summer

mid-season

winter

double-skin facade
-in summer it allows for
natural ventilation by opening
windows in the inner skin

double-skin facade
-in mid-seasons the
natural ventilation is
controlled by adjustable
louvres in between the skins

double-skin facade
-in winter the louvre
shelters the cavity becomes an
insolating cushion of air

open

open

closed

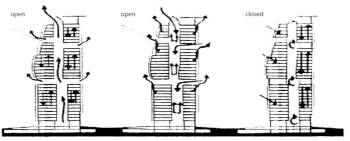

the central atrium extending over
several floors enables cross-ventilation
of the building & therefor the natural
ventilation of the office spaces & hotel
corridor next to the atria

mid-seasons: natural ventilation
to be enhanced & controlled by:
- thermal stack effects by
  thermal flue (atrium)
- wind suction

in the winter there is minimum
mechanical air supply the louvres
inside the double-skin facade are
closed in order to insulate the
building with air cavity

Legend

12   Vertical Circulation

13   Skycourt/garden

14   Public space/realm

15   Weather shield

16   Ecological chart

Shanghai Armoury Tower

Idaman Residence

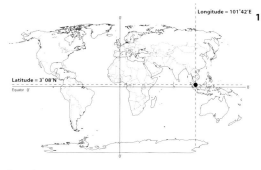

Longitude = 101°42'E

1

Latitude = 3° 08'N
Equator 0'

Location
Kuala Lumpur

Climatic Zone
Tropical

Vegetation Zone
Rainforest

No. of Storeys
34

Areas
GFA   : 39,346 sq.m.
NFA   : 31,663 sq.m.

Site Area
6,058 sq.m.

Plot Ratio
1:6.5

2

4

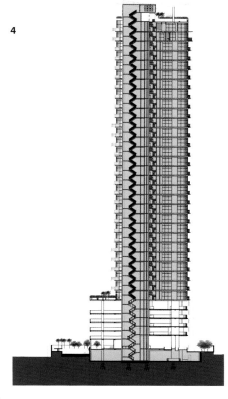

3

This is a residential tower in the central business district of Kuala Lumpur. The project introduces an integrated working and living environment in the heart of the city instead of two separate surburban zones of living and city offices.

Skycourts and terraces are introduced within the tower which provides an internal to external buffer zone and generates the microclimate at the building's preiphery. The space between the two seperate L form of the towers provides a large central atrium and with vertical separation at the corners enables a free air flow within the building to provide all units with natural ventilation.

The form of the building is shaped to allow maximum views while maintaining a naturally vented internal atrium space and core. The plan is split in two to allow cross- ventilation as well as an internal stack effect. As a result, every room, toilet and kitchen in each apartment is naturally ventilated. The atrium is column free with planted corridors linking each unit to the lift lobby.

Idaman Residence

Legend
1 Site plan
2 Landscaped terraces at level 6
3 Sun path diagram
4 Cross-section
5 View of pool corridor
6 Night view
7 Swimming pool at water wall
8 Main entrance drop-off

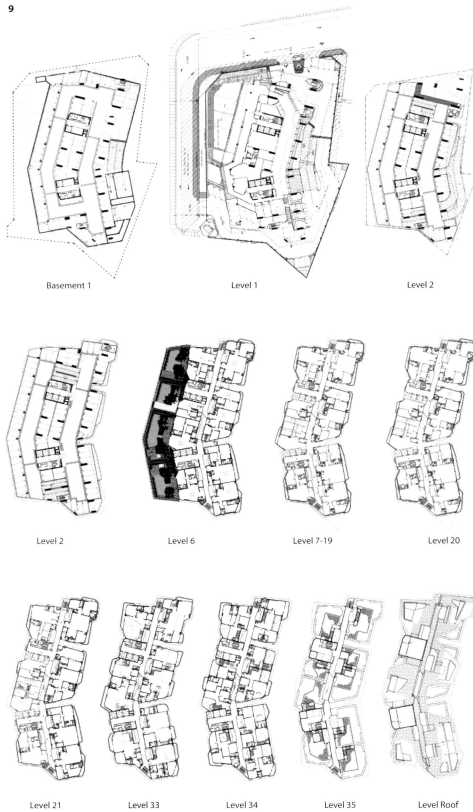

Basement 1

Level 1

Level 2

Level 2

Level 6

Level 7-19

Level 20

Level 21

Level 33

Level 34

Level 35

Level Roof

Roof garden to reduce run off and to enhance biodiversity

Wind funnel feature to naturally ventilate apartment units and internal passageways

Sunshading to protect building from hot east and west sun reduce energy consumption by air conditioning

Water wall at entrance lobby and pool side to cool microclimate

Mixed Mode cooling fans at Level 1

Vegetated opened ramp creating pool of light directing people to ground level

Idaman Residence

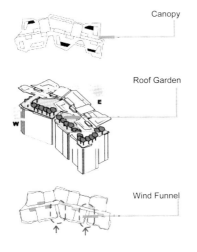

Canopy

Roof Garden

Wind Funnel

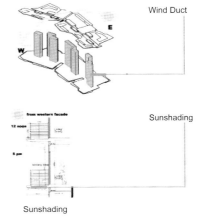

Wind Duct

from western facade

12 noon

5 pm

Sunshading

Sunshading

Legend

9 Summary of plans

10 Bioclimatic features

11

View of External Evaporative Cooling Wall

12

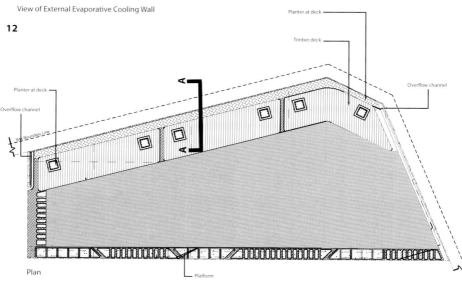

Planter at deck

Timber deck

Overflow channel

Planter at deck

Overflow channel

Site Boundary Line

Plan

Platform

13

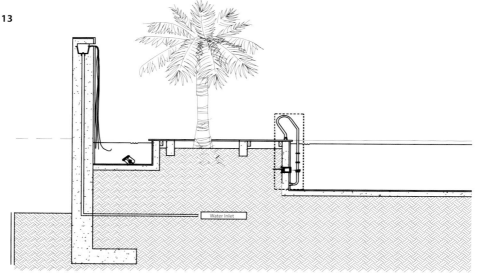

Water Inlet

Section AA

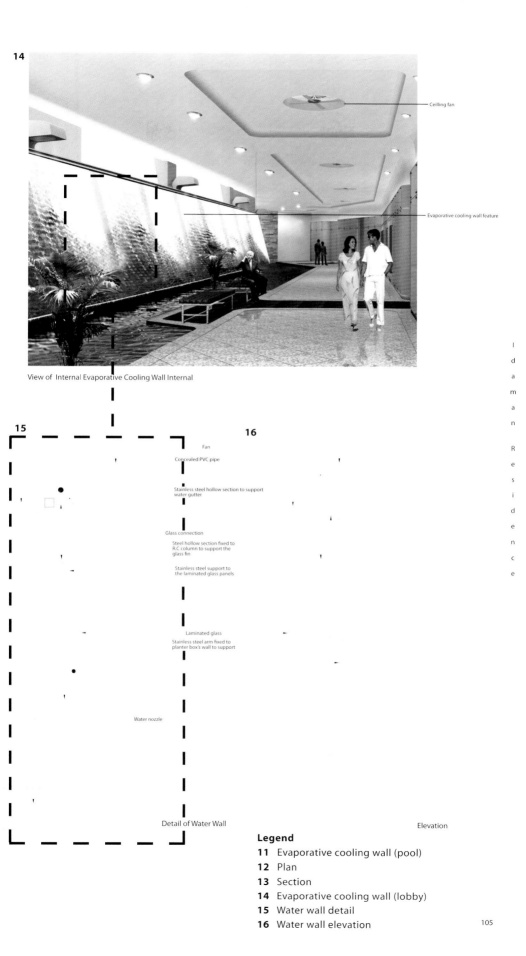

14

Ceilling fan

Evaporative cooling wall feature

View of Internal Evaporative Cooling Wall Internal

15

16

Fan

Concealed PVC pipe

Stainless steel hollow section to support
water gutter

Glass connection

Steel hollow section fixed to
R.C column to support the
glass fin

Stainless steel support to
the laminated glass panels

Laminated glass
Stainless steel arm fixed to
planter box's wall to support

Water nozzle

Detail of Water Wall

Elevation

Legend

11 Evaporative cooling wall (pool)
12 Plan
13 Section
14 Evaporative cooling wall (lobby)
15 Water wall detail
16 Water wall elevation

MAAG Tower

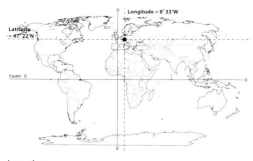

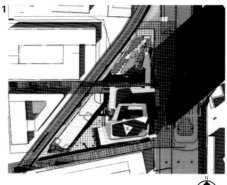

Location
Zurich

Climatic Zone
Cold

Vegetation Zone
Alpine

No. of Storeys
34

Areas
GFA   : 47,788 sq.m.
NFA   : 35,841 sq.m.

Site Area
5,487 sq.m.

Plot Ratio
1 : 9

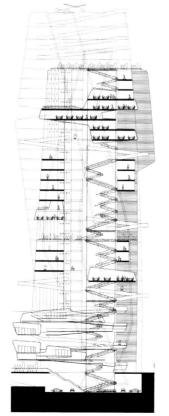

4

3

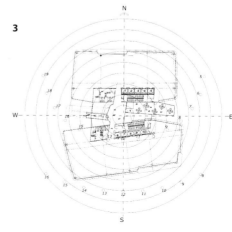

The tower responds to the changing seasons of the locality in terms of temperature, wind and sun. The inner courtyards and winter gardens, integrated with the façades, are the primary design features to optimise its performance.

The main ecological feature of the tower is its green lung in the form of a central shaft. Apart from providing a healthier quality of air, this core is used to integrate bio-mass to balance the building's inorganic content and also to increase the locality's biodiversity. The concept of a multiuse ecological zone as an 'eco-cell' is introduced in this building by providing continuous landscaping that extends from the basement up to the top of tower. The design also uses green materials in its construction and structure.

The approach to the lighting design is to maximise daylight into deeper areas of the floor plate by vertical fibre optic daylight tubes and holographic sunshades at the north - east and south - west façades. This optimisation of passive mode design strategies provides adequate shading during the summer and maximum solar entry in winter. The 'green pockets' and eco-vegetation wall within the tower are not only an ecological response but also provide a 'stress-less' bioclimatic environment.

5

6

Legend
1 Site plan
2 Elevation
3 Sun path diagram
4 Cross-section
5 South east view
6 Aerial view of the model

7

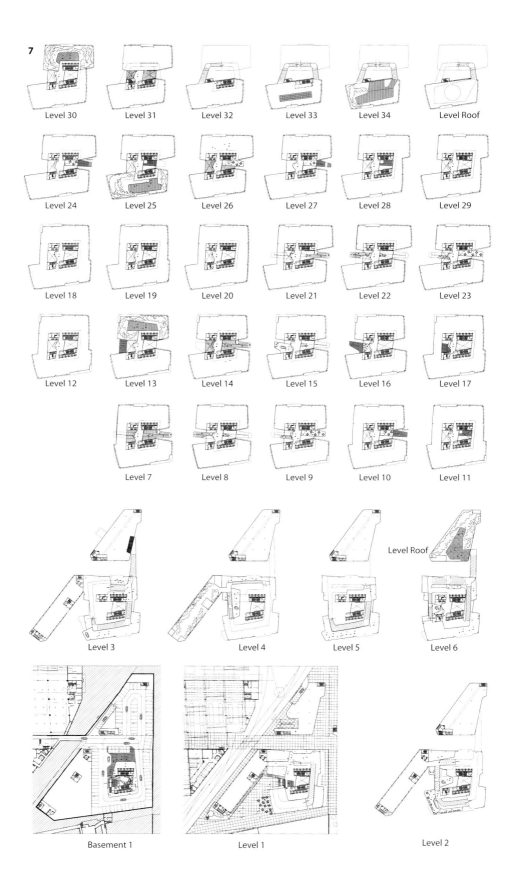

Level 30 Level 31 Level 32 Level 33 Level 34 Level Roof

Level 24 Level 25 Level 26 Level 27 Level 28 Level 29

Level 18 Level 19 Level 20 Level 21 Level 22 Level 23

Level 12 Level 13 Level 14 Level 15 Level 16 Level 17

Level 7 Level 8 Level 9 Level 10 Level 11

Level Roof

Level 3 Level 4 Level 5 Level 6

Basement 1 Level 1 Level 2

8

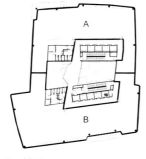

Single Tenancy

GFA=1488.67sq.m.
NFA=1402.15sq.m.

Efficiency: 9 4%

9

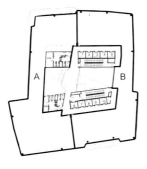

Double Tenancy

GFA=1488.67sq.m.
NFA=1130.29sq.m.

Efficiency: 7 6%

10

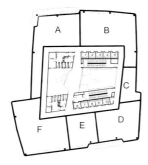

Double Tenancy

GFA=1488.67sq.m.
NFA=1130.29sq.m.

Efficiency: 7 6%

11

Multiple Tenancy

GFA=1488.67sq.m.
NFA=965.79sq.m.

Efficiency: 6 5%

12

M
A
A
G

T
o
w
e
r

13

Legend
7 Summary of plans
8 Single tenancy
9 Double tenancy A
10 Double tenancy B
11 Multiple tenancy
12 South view
13 View of the roof-top garden

14

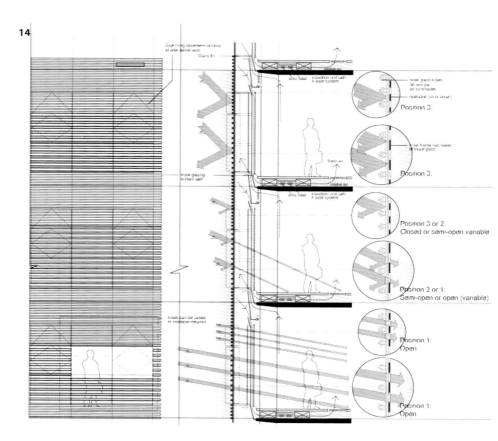

15

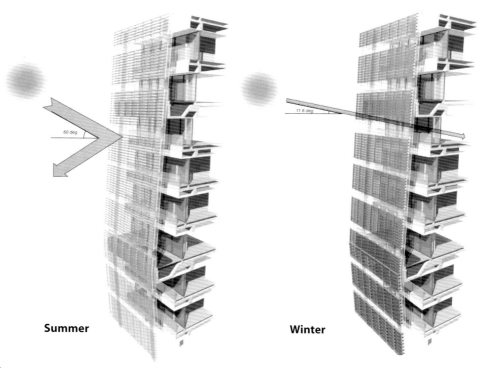

Summer

Winter

16

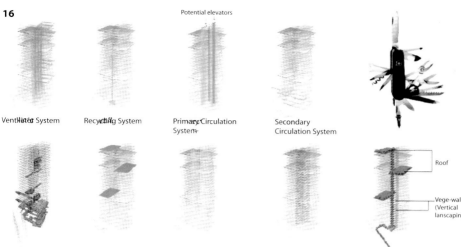

Potential elevators

Ventilator System   Recycling System   Primary Circulation System   Secondary Circulation System

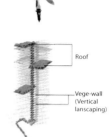

Tertiary Circulation System   Water Recycling System   Daylight System   Staircase   Vertical Landscaping

Roof

Vege-wall (Vertical lanscaping)

17

Legend
14 Sunshading diagram 1
15 Sunshading diagram 2
16 Tower features diagram
17 View of top of tower

Al-Asima Shopping Village Tower

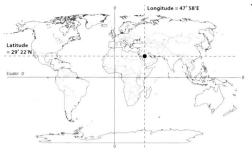

Location
Kuwait

Climatic Zone
Dry

Vegetation Zone
Desert-scrub

No. of Storeys
Signature Office Tower = 40
Independant Office block = 4
Podium Shopping block = 3

Areas
GFA   : 140,460 sq.m.
NFA   : 102,000 sq.m.

Site Area
44,000 sq.m.

Plot Ratio
1 : 3.2

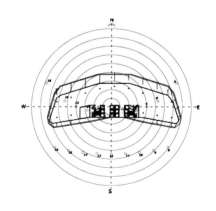

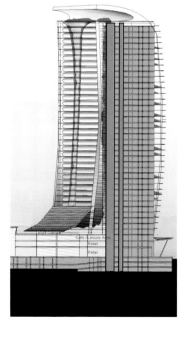

The tower's podium is conceptually three village clusters, each containing a glass roof providing day light to its central courtyard. A 'V' form central plaza unites the clusters at the confluence of the internal streets, which link the three main pedestrian entrances. On the corner is a slim office tower with bioclimatic features. The main office floors face north for waterfront views, with slim east and west facades to reduce solar gain, and the major service and elevator cores shield the southern roof-podium.

The green features of this building include a landscaped forecourt to the main retail entrance at Level 1, vegetated ramps from the plaza to Level 3 roof terrace, internal ramps with cascading water feature at Level 3, sky terraces with planting at Level 26 and a vegetated roof garden. The southern façade is also veiled with a planted green layer and the façade incorporates sky terraces with planting. A series of responsive shading devices are provided on the tower and natural ventilation is provided to the shopping streets by an operable roof. Water management collection, irrigation and planting and the recycling of waste are also included. Evaporative cooling towers enhance internal air - movement and cooling.

5

6

7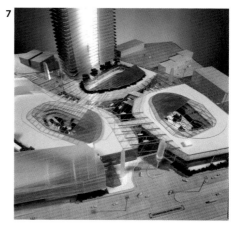

8

Legend
1 Site plan
2 South east view
3 Sun path diagram
4 Cross-Section
5 Aerial view from west
6 Aerial view from south
7 Aerial view from north
8 View of main entrance

9

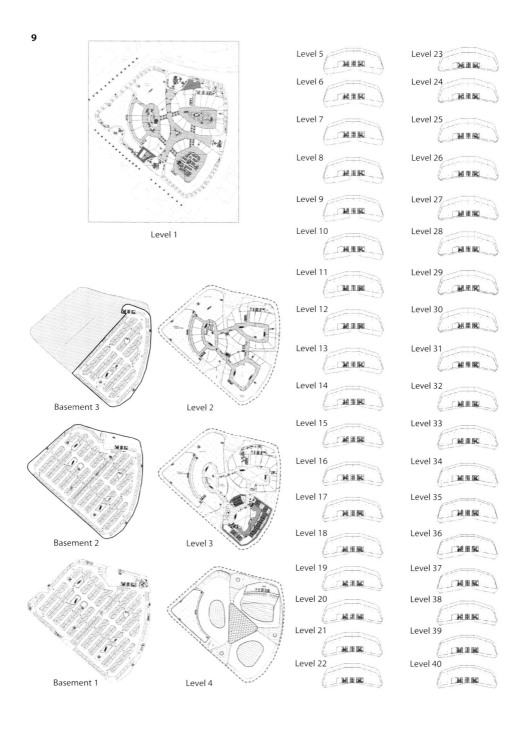

Level 1

Basement 3

Level 2

Basement 2

Level 3

Basement 1

Level 4

Level 5
Level 6
Level 7
Level 8
Level 9
Level 10
Level 11
Level 12
Level 13
Level 14
Level 15
Level 16
Level 17
Level 18
Level 19
Level 20
Level 21
Level 22

Level 23
Level 24
Level 25
Level 26
Level 27
Level 28
Level 29
Level 30
Level 31
Level 32
Level 33
Level 34
Level 35
Level 36
Level 37
Level 38
Level 39
Level 40

Summary of Plans

Legend
9 Summary of plans
10 View from south west
11 Aerial view
12 The plaza

The Residence - TTDI Phase 6D1

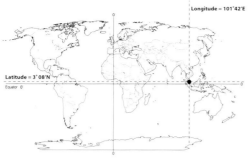

Longitude = 101°42'E

Latitude = 3°08'N

Equator 0°

1

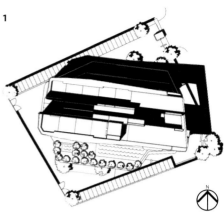

N

Location
Kuala Lumpur

Climatic Zone
Tropical

Vegetation Zone
Rainforest

No. of Storeys
21

Areas
GFA   : 27,800 sq.m.
NFA   : 20,850 sq.m.

Site Area
6,070 sq.m.

Plot Ratio
1:5

2

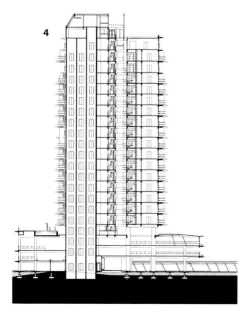

4

3

The tower's design originates from the idea of a series of internal air wells combined with a wind-scoop at the base of the tower to ventilate the inner parts of the floor plate and to improve internal comfort conditions. The built form is orientated north - south for optimal solar performance. The penthouses consist of three stepped terraces which overlook the park, and are shaded by a canopy. The common facilities are located at Level 4 with an infinity pool overlooking the park to the north - east.

CFD analyses was carried out to understand the sunlight penetration, solar gain and surface temperature rise inside the dwelling units in the course of the day. The east - west façade is sun-shaded to protect direct sun entering into the internal spaces until 4pm. The sun-shades are based on a sun path study and the sun angles on the façade.

The tower is orientated north-south to maximise the view towards the nearby golf club and forest reserve and for optimal solar performance. The wing walls are introduced into the façade as wind scoops. Natural ventilation is maximised throughout the entire building. Floor voids channel wind upwards and the wind flow to internal passageways further helps ventilate the rear walls and internal spaces of the dwelling units. These passive mode strategies result in a low energy consumption building while providing user comfort.

5

6

7

Legend
1 Site plan
2 Aerial view
3 Sun path diagram
4 Cross-section
5 Main entrance
6 Canopy
7 Pool

8

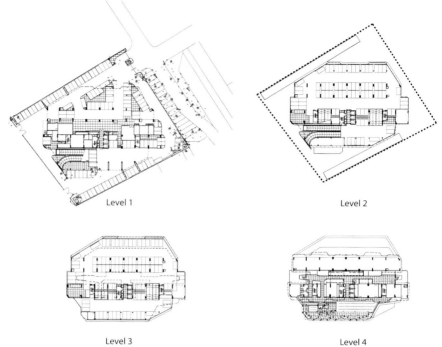

Level 1

Level 2

Level 3

Level 4

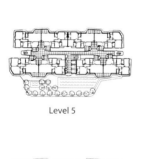

Level 5

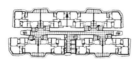

Level 6 to 11 (typical)

Level 12 & 13

Level 15 to 18

Level 19

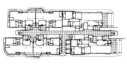

Level 20 (lower Penthouse)

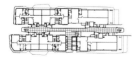

Level 21 (Upper Penthouse)

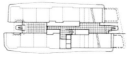

Lower Roof Plan

Upper Roof Plan

9

With shading. Without Shading.

Sunshade essential as shown by these simulations of daylight penetrations into north facade apartments in 6D (1) (with and without sun shading)

Without shading. With Shading.

Sunlight penetrations of south facade apartments in 6D (1) with and without shading

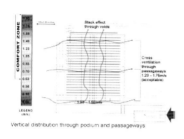

Vertical distribution through podium and passageways

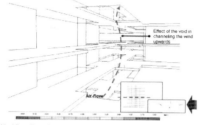

Wind flow through passageways and voids

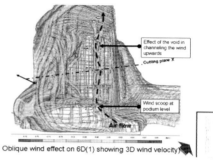

Oblique wind effect on 6D(1) showing 3D wind velocity

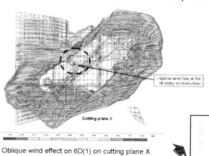

Oblique wind effect on 6D(1) on cutting plane X

10

11

12

Legend

8 Summary of plans
9 CFD analysis diagrams
10 North west-view
11 Overlay terrace
12 Swimming pool

The Plaza - TTDI Phase 6D3

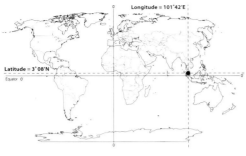

Location
Kuala Lumpur

Climatic Zone
Tropical

Vegetation Zone
Rainforest

No. of Storeys
29

Areas
GFA   : 61,635 sq.m.
NFA   : 46,226 sq.m.

Site Area
13,635 sq.m.

Plot Ratio
1:4.5

1

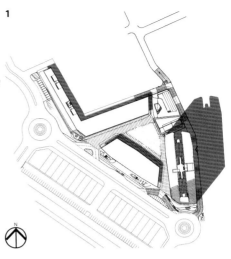

2

4

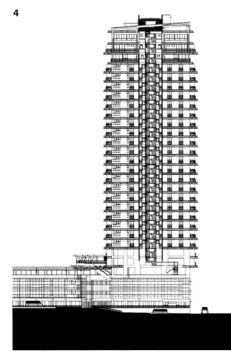

3

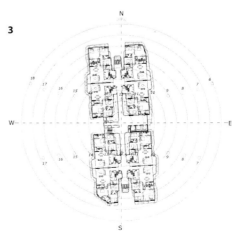

The tower's built form is orientated to maximise the views towards the city, the nearby golf club and the forest reserve.

The central multi - use retail plaza is a mixed mode naturally ventilated atrium with a large canopy whose internal comfort conditions and natural ventilation are moderated by three industrial size extraction fans. Common facilities are located at level 4 of the plaza and a pool overlooks the park on the north - east. The corridors of the apartments are naturally ventilated by induction of air from level 4 up to the roof level. The skycourts located at level 28 are vegetated. The plaza has a three Eco-Cells that extends down to the basement areas.

5

6

8

7

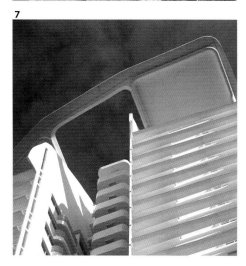

Legend
1 Site plan
2 View from south - west
3 Sun path diagram
4 Cross-section
5 Aerial view from north - east
6 Worm's eye view
7 Roof canopy
8 Plaza shoplots

Basement 1

Basement 2

Basement 3

Level 1

Level 2

Level 3

Level 4

Level 5

Level 6   Level 7-15 & Level 18-26   Level 28   Level 28M

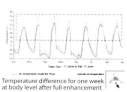

Building context and location

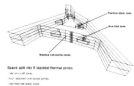

Model used for analysis

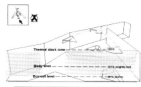

Temperature difference for one week
at body level after full enhancement

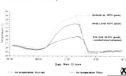

Temperature difference at body
level at concourse and eco-cell
location without extractor-fan

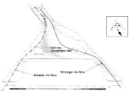

Temperature at body level with air extractor off
(vertical view)

Temperature at body level with air extractor on
(vertical view)

Simulation using external CFD: air flow through the plaza
(plan view)

Air flow thourgh the plaza (vertical view A)

Design enhancements to improve comfort conditions

1. Shop-lot parapet-wall raised 1.2m to underneath canopy
2. Stack-roof extended 1.0m above canopy
3. Skylight-glass to be low-e glass

Isothermal visualization showing boundry condition indicating
combined temperature of surfaces and air movement

Temperature at body level with air extractor
off at 2pm (plan view)

Temperature at body level with extractor on
(plan view)

Temperature at body level comparing with air-extractor
off and air-extractor on (vertical view)

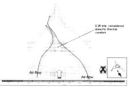

Simulation using external cfd: Air movement at body
level with perpendicular wind

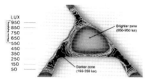

Simulation of internal lighting levels in the Plaza (plan) using low-e
glass (isolux image) using Radiance software (plan view)

Effective internal lighting conditions (isolux image)
in the Plaza using low-e glass usng Radiance software

UMNO Tower

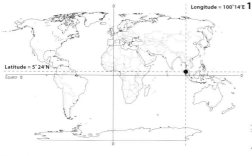

Longitude = 100°14'E **1**

Latitude = 5° 24'N
Equator 0

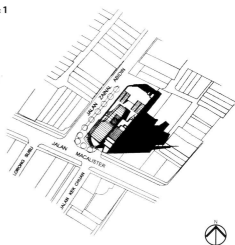

N

Location
Penang

Climatic Zone
Tropical

Vegetation Zone
Rainforest

No. of Storeys
21

Areas
GFA   : 10,900 sq.m.
NFA   : 8,192 sq.m.

Site Area
1,920 sq.m.

Plot Ratio
1 : 5.5

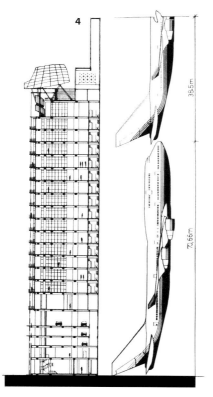

2

4

38.5m

72.66m

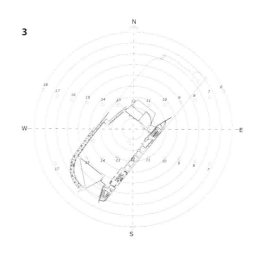

3

The built form of the tower takes the familiar format of a base, with a banking hall, an auditorium and car-parking levels, a main body with 14 floors of office space and a penthouse.

The plan - form makes the best of a restricted narrow corner site with a wall of elevators, services and staircases that form a tall party-wall facing east/south - east, defending the internal spaces from solar gain. The opposite west/north - west facade is glazed and shielded with solar-orientated horizontal shades.

Relative to the wind-rose and prevailing winds, are the soaring vertical fins that serve as wind wing-walls' to deflect and direct wind through balcony zones. These create wind pockets with 'air locks' via full height sliding-doors providing natural ventilation into the internal office space.

5

6

7

Legend
1 Site plan
2 View from Jalan Macalister
3 Sun path diagram
4 Cross-section
5 View from south
6 View from south-west
7 Aerial view

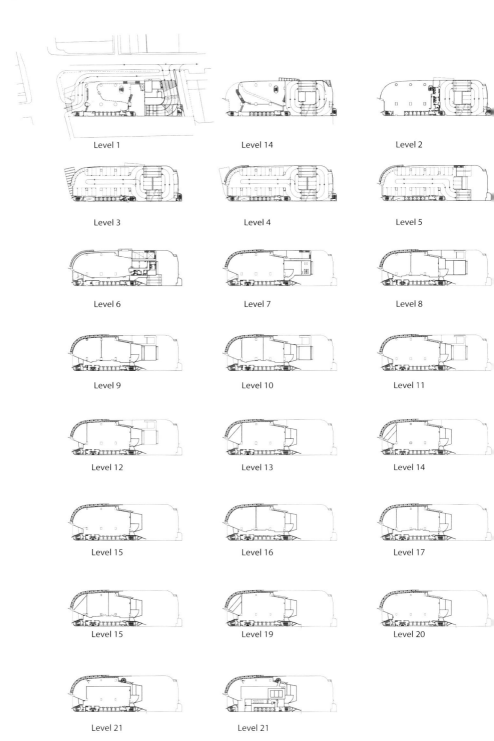

Level 1

Level 14

Level 2

Level 3

Level 4

Level 5

Level 6

Level 7

Level 8

Level 9

Level 10

Level 11

Level 12

Level 13

Level 14

Level 15

Level 16

Level 17

Level 15

Level 19

Level 20

Level 21

Level 21

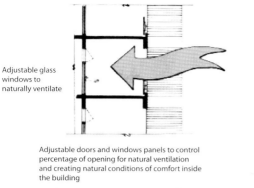

Adjustable glass windows to naturally ventilate

Adjustable doors and windows panels to control percentage of opening for natural ventilation and creating natural conditions of comfort inside the building

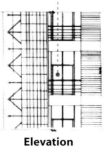

Elevation

Aluminium Louvered Plant Room

A   A

Openable Balcony Door

Wind Pocket - Balcony

Wing Wall

Detail of Wind Pocket

11

10

12 Noon

3 PM

6 PM

A ⌐ A

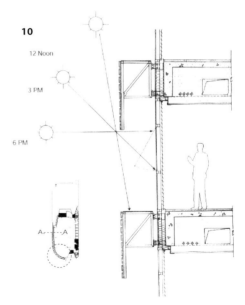

Legend
8 Summary of plans
9 Detail of wind pocket
10 View of wind wall
11 Sunshading diagram

11

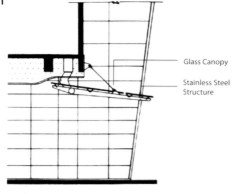

Glass Canopy

Stainless Steel
Structure

Canopy - Section

Glass Canopy

Stainless Steel
Structure

Canopy - Plan

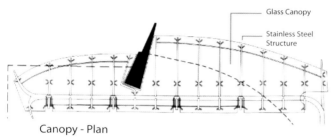

12

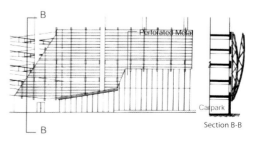

Perforated Metal

Carpark

Section B-B

Perforated Metal Sunshades

13

16

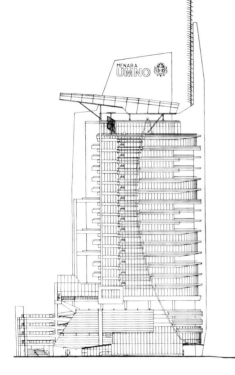

14

15

Legend

11 Canopy diagram
12 Perforated metal sunshade
13 Night view
14 View from south-east
15 View from south
16 Elevation from Jalan Zainal Abidin

Nagoya EXPO Tower

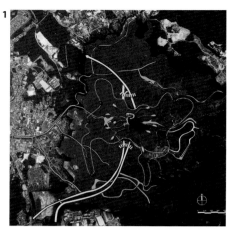

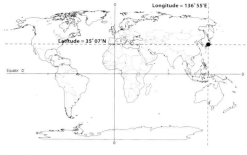

Location
Nagoya

Climatic Zone
Cold

Vegetation Zone
Deciduous Forest

No. of Storeys
50

Areas
GFA   : 902,458 sq.m.
NFA   : 631,316 sq.m.

Site Area
607, 035 sq.m.

Plot Ratio
1 : 5

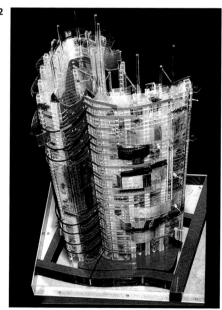

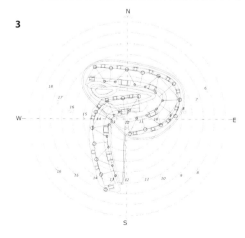

The tower's vertical strategy with its triangular mega-structure and horizontal cross bracing, is similar to the Tokyo-Nara Tower. In this case, the structural floors form 'land-in-the-sky' for construction of offices, light industry, residential units, urban infrastructure, exposition pavilions, hotels and commercial units.

The tower has multiple vertical circulation systems including an internal spiral Mass Transit System that has stations at intermittent intervals.

The proposal for vertical expo is to avoid building extensively over an ecologically sensitive site.

This tower has multiple vegetation zones which consist of the Main Park 1, Main Park 2 and Sky Park 3. Apart from these, there are thematic gardens and ramp parks. To this mix is added a host of facilities including an arts and crafts village, convention hall and theatres. The main U-form of the curved plan is orientated to acquire views and natural light, with vistas that include Mount Fuji and the Nagoya Bay Ise Shrine.

5

6

Vertical Expo 2005 Prototype Hypertower

Total Area of Site	- 540ha	100.0 %
Proposed Area of Development	- 150ha	27.7 %
Proposed Footprint @ 50 Segments	- 150 / 50	
	= 3ha	0.5 %
Area Reserved for Natural Environment	- 537ha	99.5 %
Increase in Area Saved for Natural Environment	- 147ha	27.2 %

3ha

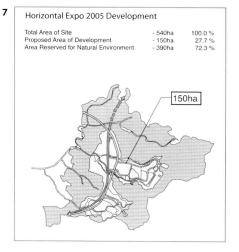

7

Horizontal Expo 2005 Development

Total Area of Site	- 540ha	100.0 %
Proposed Area of Development	- 150ha	27.7 %
Area Reserved for Natural Environment	- 390ha	72.3 %

150ha

Legend

1 Site plan
2 Aerial view
3 Sun path diagram
4 Cross-section
5 General view
6 Footprint of vertical EXPO compared with horizontal EXPO

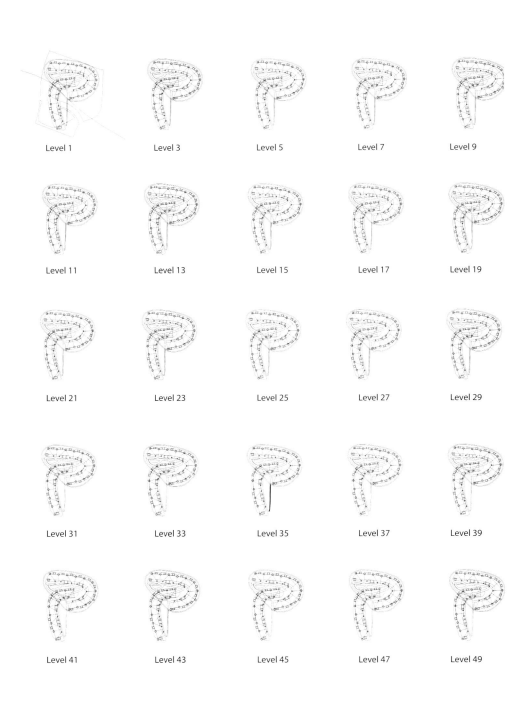

Level 1

Level 3

Level 5

Level 7

Level 9

Level 11

Level 13

Level 15

Level 17

Level 19

Level 21

Level 23

Level 25

Level 27

Level 29

Level 31

Level 33

Level 35

Level 37

Level 39

Level 41

Level 43

Level 45

Level 47

Level 49

9

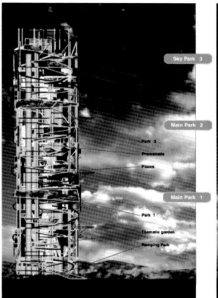

Sky Park 3

Main Park 2

Park 3
Promenade
Piazza

Main Park 1

Park 1
Thematic garden
Ramping Park

10

Helipad
Public Observation Deck

Refuge Zone

Pedestrian Ramp

LRT Stations

International Pavilions
Arts and Crafts Village

Refuge Zone

Japanese Pavilions

International
Pavilions

International
Organization Zone

Administrator

Refuge Zone

International Pavilions

Convention Hall

Auditorium

Amphitheater

Parking Facilities

Refuge Zone

11

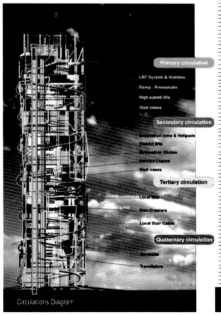

Primary circulation

LRT System & Stations
Ramp - Promenade
High speed lifts
Stair cases

Secondary circulation

Evacuation zone & Helipads
District lifts
Evacuation Chutes
Gondola Cranes
Stair cases

Tertiary circulation

Local lifts
Skin Crawlers
Local Stair Cases

Quaternary circulation

Gondolas
Travellators

Circulations Diagram

12

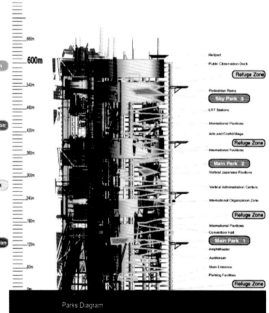

600m

660m
540m
480m
420m
360m
300m
240m
180m
120m
60m

Helipad
Public Observation Deck

Refuge Zone

Pedestrian Ramp

Sky Park 3

LRT Stations

International Pavilions
Arts and Crafts Village

Refuge Zone

International Pavilions

Main Park 2

Vertical Japanese Pavilions

Vertical Administration Centers

International Organization Zone

Refuge Zone

International Pavilions
Convention Hall

Main Park 1

Amphitheater
Auditorium

Main Entrance

Parking Facilities

Refuge Zone

Parks Diagram

Legend

8 Summary of plans
9 Green features diagram
10 Programme diagram
11 Circulation diagram
12 Elevation

13

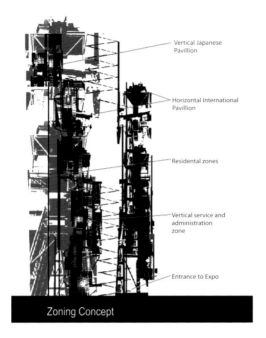

Vertical Japanese Pavillion

Horizontal International Pavillion

Residental zones

Vertical service and administration zone

Entrance to Expo

Zoning Concept

14

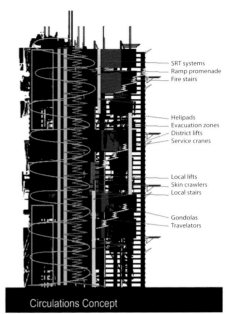

SRT systems
Ramp promenade
Fire stairs

Helipads
Evacuation zones
District lifts
Service cranes

Local lifts
Skin crawlers
Local stairs

Gondolas
Travelators

Circulations Concept

15

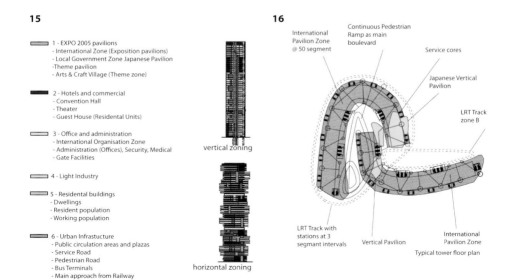

1 - EXPO 2005 pavilions
- International Zone (Exposition pavilions)
- Local Government Zone Japanese Pavilion
- Theme pavilion
- Arts & Craft Village (Theme zone)

2 - Hotels and commercial
- Convention Hall
- Theater
- Guest House (Residental Units)

3 - Office and administration
- International Organisation Zone
- Administration (Offices), Security, Medical
- Gate Facilities

4 - Light Industry

5 - Residental buildings
- Dwellings
- Resident population
- Working population

6 - Urban Infrastucture
- Public circulation areas and plazas
- Service Road
- Pedestrian Road
- Bus Terminals
- Main approach from Railway
- Main approach from Bus
- Arterial road
- Moving Walk

vertical zoning

horizontal zoning

Tower Programs

16

International Pavilion Zone @ 50 segment

Continuous Pedestrian Ramp as main boulevard

Service cores

Japanese Vertical Pavilion

LRT Track zone B

LRT Track with stations at 3 segment intervals

Vertical Pavilion

International Pavilion Zone

Typical tower floor plan

Tower Features

17

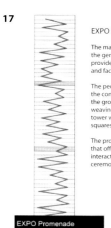

EXPO Promenade

The main feature of the EXPO 2005 tower will be the gentle vertically accesible promenade which provide access to all the pavilions, public areas and facilities.

The pedestrian promenade takes the form of the continuous looping ramp traversing from the ground paine to the top of the tower, weaving together the different parts of the tower where secondary streets and public squares may extend off this public realms.

The promenade loop have points of intersection that offer a potential territory of dynamic urban interaction, activities and expo-related ceremonies.

EXPO Promenade

18

Secondary Circulation

The secondary circulation system provides the links between each of the three hyperzones using secondary 'district' lifts, evacuation paths, escalators, ramps and staircases.

	district lifts
	evacuation paths

Secondary Circulation

19

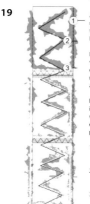

Vegetation Strategy

As the 2005 Expo is held over the summer months, the weather would be ideal to enable the profuse use of local plant types and strategic landscaping within the tower.

In addition to decorative and ceremonial uses, vegetation becomes an integral part of the external facade system for sunshading and micro-climatic control (particularly the hot east and west sides).

Pocket of lush grennery placed at regular intervals along the entire height of the tower, will serve as green lungs refreshing the environment, improving the air quality and provide:

1   vegetation on the facade for sunshading and micro-climatic control

2   decorative landscaping along the main exposition promenade

3   vegetation pockets located in public areas as natural air fresheners.

Vegetation Strategy

20

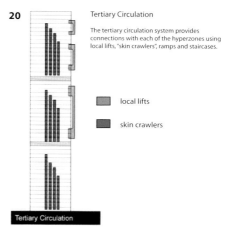

Tertiary Circulation

The tertiary circulation system provides connections with each of the hyperzones using local lifts, "skin crawlers", ramps and staircases.

	local lifts
	skin crawlers

Tertiary Circulation

Nagoya EXPO Tower

21

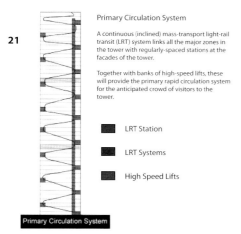

Primary Circulation System

A continuous (inclined) mass-transport light-rail transit (LRT) system links all the major zones in the tower with regularly-spaced stations at the facades of the tower.

Together with banks of high-speed lifts, these will provide the primary rapid circulation system for the anticipated crowd of visitors to the tower.

	LRT Station
	LRT Systems
	High Speed Lifts

Primary Circulation System

22

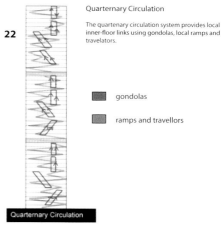

Quarternary Circulation

The quarternary circulation system provides local inner-floor links using gondolas, local ramps and travelators.

	gondolas
	ramps and travellors

Quarternary Circulation

Legend

Yee Nen Tower

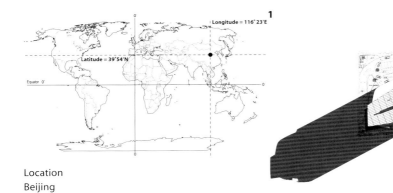

1

Longitude = 116° 23'E

Latitude = 39°54'N

Equator 0°

N

Location
Beijing

Climatic Zone
Cold

Vegetation Zone
Deciduous Forest

No. of Storeys
25

Areas
GFA   : 72,550 sq.m.
NFA   : 54,412 sq.m.

Site Area
5,600 sq.m.

Plot Ratio
1 : 8.8

2

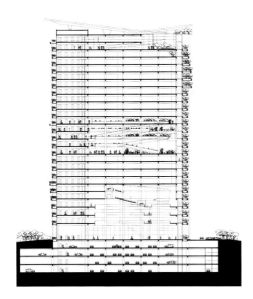

4

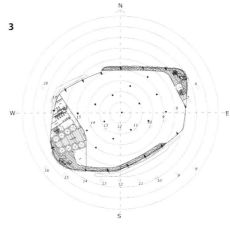

3

The functions in the tower are mainly for office use, with retail spaces, some public facilities, and supporting facilities for the children centre such as a multi-purpose hall.

The key feature is the light pipes incorporated in the façade which throw daylight into the inner parts of the floor plate without the use of any electricity.

The landscaped public areas contain community spaces for various public activities such as café, gym, games room and reading areas.

The plaza level is raised 1m above street level with parts of the site's boundaries mounded up to +2.0m, gradually stepping down with water features and terraces towards the tower base. This gives the impression from the ramp approaching the tower that the office tower is sitting in a landscaped valley.

Within the landscaped areas there are several Eco-Cells, designed to bring daylight and natural ventilation into the basement levels below, offering safer and more cheerful underground experience.

The tower is orientated to the South-East and North-West to avoid extreme solar heat gains during summer seasons. All lift lobbies and escape staircases can be naturally lit and ventilated.

Sun shading devices are introduced to minimize direct heat gain by sun light into the office space in summer, but to capture the low winter sun. The floor plates of the office levels are designed with an efficiency of 81%, while maintaining city views with landscaped sky terraces, roof gardens and a viewing platform.

5

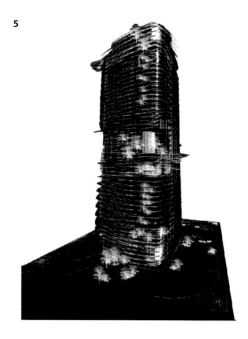

6

Yeen Nen Tower

Legend
1 Site plan
2 Aerial view
3 Sun path diagram
4 Cross-section
5 Eye-level view
6 Facade showing light-pipes

7

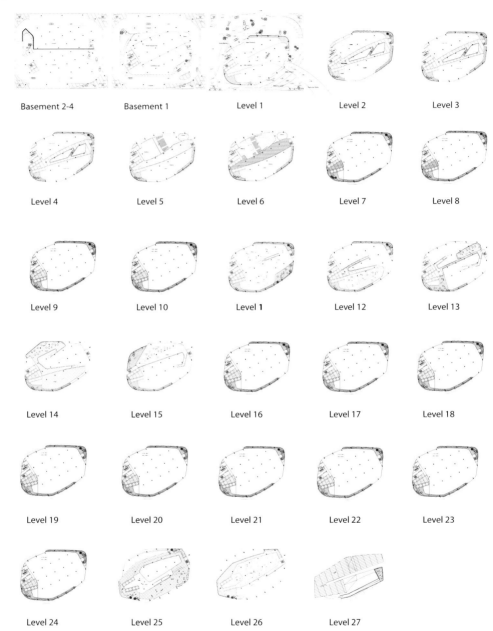

Basement 2-4

Basement 1

Level 1

Level 2

Level 3

Level 4

Level 5

Level 6

Level 7

Level 8

Level 9

Level 10

Level 1

Level 12

Level 13

Level 14

Level 15

Level 16

Level 17

Level 18

Level 19

Level 20

Level 21

Level 22

Level 23

Level 24

Level 25

Level 26

Level 27

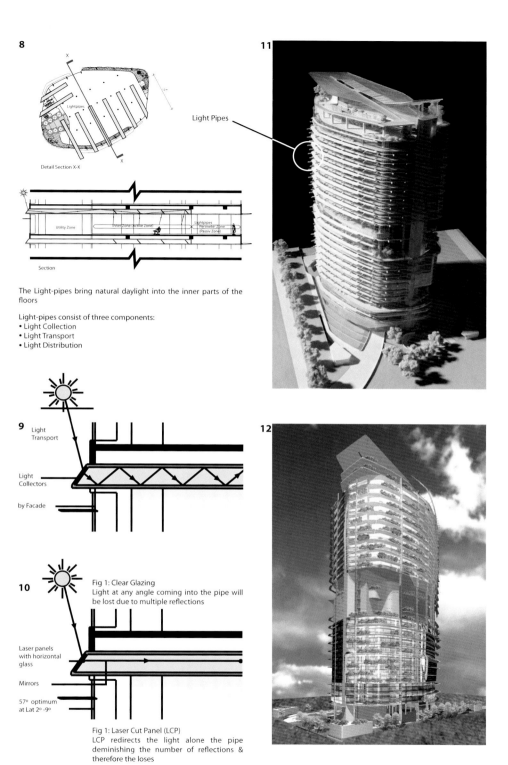

8

Detail Section X-X

Lightpipes

Section

Utility Zone — Inner Zone (Active Zone) — Lightpipes Perimeter Zone (Passiv Zone)

The Light-pipes bring natural daylight into the inner parts of the floors

Light-pipes consist of three components:
• Light Collection
• Light Transport
• Light Distribution

9 Light Transport

Light Collectors

by Facade

10

Fig 1: Clear Glazing
Light at any angle coming into the pipe will be lost due to multiple reflections

Laser panels with horizontal glass

Mirrors

57° optimum at Lat 2° -9°

Fig 1: Laser Cut Panel (LCP)
LCP redirects the light alone the pipe deminishing the number of reflections & therefore the loses

11 Light Pipes

12

Yeen Nen Tower

Legend

7 Summary of plans
8 Light pipes layout at ceiling
9 Light pipe cross-section showing Laser Cut panel
10 LCP diagram
11 View from south-east
12 Worm's eye view

Reliance Tower

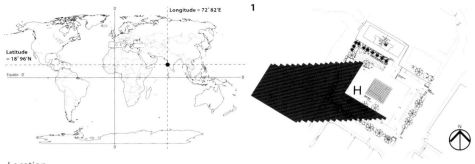

1

Location
Mumbai

Climatic Zone
Tropical

Vegetation Zone
Rainforest

No. of Storeys
25

Areas
GFA   : 28,850 sq.m.
NFA   : 21,638 sq.m.

Site Area
4,324 sq.m.

Plot Ratio
1:6

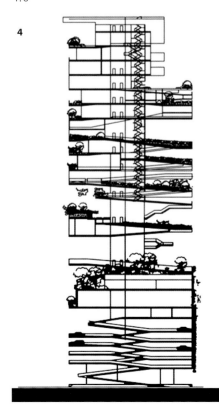

2

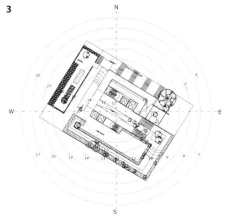

4

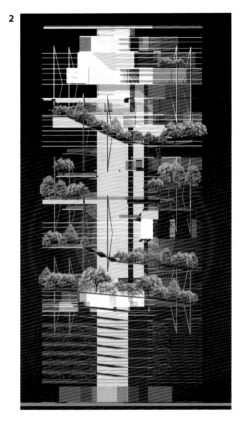

3

This residential tower sits in the heart of the heavily populated metropolis and is primarily a home for a single family. The tower height is 150 metres above sea level, higher than the other high – rise buildings in the area.

The height maximises views that the site offers on all sides especially views out to the sea. The residence was designed essentially as a 'normal home' with 'generational interaction' between all family members. Allowance for future extensions and the alterations in the role of individual spaces are designed in.

Landscaped garden terraces are located on each floor of the tower. These also serve as refuge floors as well as 'green lung' spaces that exploit the advantage of passive energy systems. The structure is a vertical park, with each floor exploiting an individual theme that is linked to the tower's health and recreational facilities.

5

Legend
1 Site plan
2 Elevation
3 Sun path diagram
4 Cross-section
5 Residence layouts

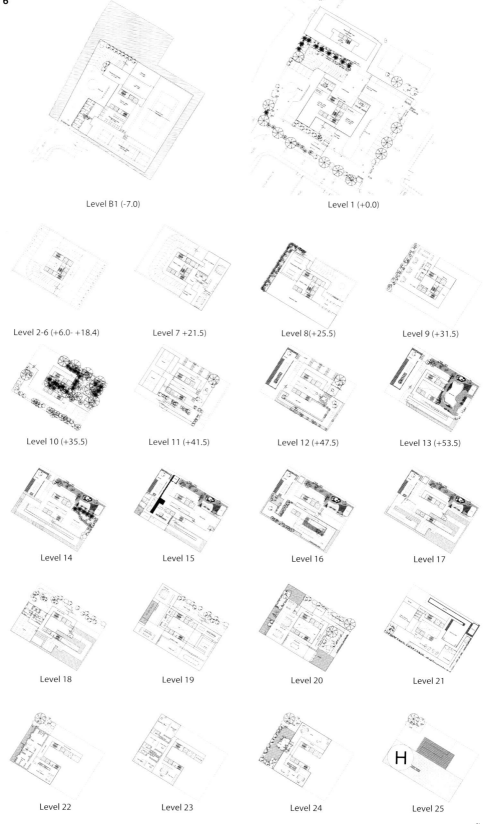

Level B1 (-7.0)

Level 1 (+0.0)

Level 2-6 (+6.0- +18.4)

Level 7 +21.5)

Level 8(+25.5)

Level 9 (+31.5)

Level 10 (+35.5)

Level 11 (+41.5)

Level 12 (+47.5)

Level 13 (+53.5)

Level 14

Level 15

Level 16

Level 17

Level 18

Level 19

Level 20

Level 21

Level 22

Level 23

Level 24

Level 25

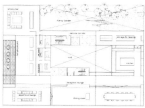

Level 19(+85.0): Formal Lounge & Dining

Level 20(+91.0): Family Lounge & Prayer Room

Level 21(+96.0): Recreation & Pool Deck

Level 22(+101.0): Children's Rooms

Level 23(+105.0): Master Bedroom

Level 4(+109.0): Master Bedroom Study Space

Residence Layouts
Conceptual design for Residence Antalia

Legend
6 Summary of plans
7 Street level view

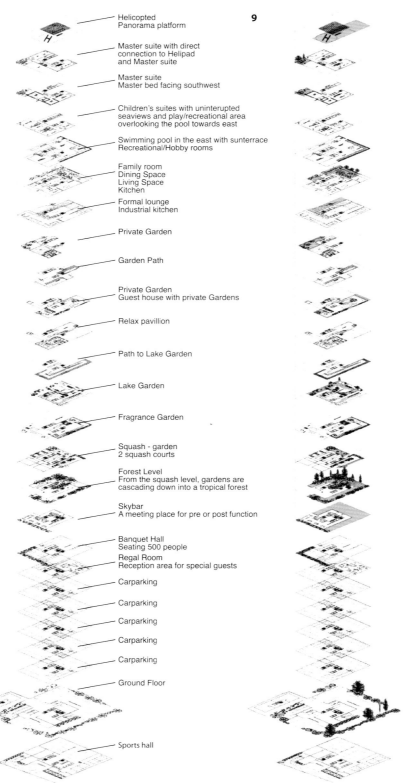

Helicopted
Panorama platform

Master suite with direct
connection to Helipad
and Master suite

Master suite
Master bed facing southwest

Children's suites with uninterupted
seaviews and play/recreational area
overlooking the pool towards east

Swimming pool in the east with sunterrace
Recreational/Hobby rooms

Family room
Dining Space
Living Space
Kitchen

Formal lounge
Industrial kitchen

Private Garden

Garden Path

Private Garden
Guest house with private Gardens

Relax pavillion

Path to Lake Garden

Lake Garden

Fragrance Garden

Squash - garden
2 squash courts

Forest Level
From the squash level, gardens are
cascading down into a tropical forest

Skybar
A meeting place for pre or post function

Banquet Hall
Seating 500 people

Regal Room
Reception area for special guests

Carparking

Carparking

Carparking

Carparking

Carparking

Ground Floor

Sports hall

Program Diagram   **Planting Diagram**

9

Legend

8 Program diagram
9 Planting diagram
10 Vertical landscaping
11 Vegetated façade

11

Santa Fe Tower

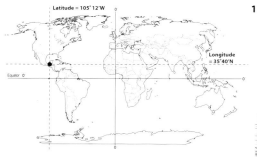

1

Location
Mexico City

Climatic Zone
Dry

Vegetation Zone
Desert-scrub

No. of Storeys
42/44

Areas
GFA   : 65,030 sq.m.
NFA   : 52,024 sq.m.

Site Area
5,946 sq.m.

Plot Ratio
1:11

2

4

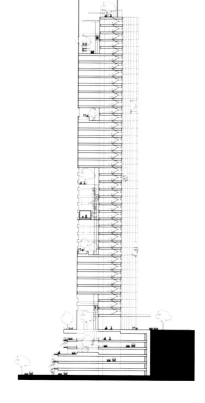

3

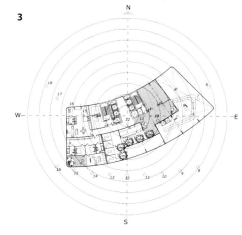

The hotel has two towers with a linked public realm. Each tower has an observation deck which allows the guests to experience panoramic view of the city from the highest point of the hotel. The hotel consists of 42-storeys with hotel suites (standard and deluxe) located at Level 6 - Level 28 while residential suites are located at Level 32- Level 42.

The internal plazas provide unique places-in-the-sky with greenery and water features placed strategically at the upper parts of the tower consisting of the Main Plaza atrium, the Lobby with courtyard atrium, the Restaurant Plaza, the Business Centre Plaza, the Infinity Pool and Fitness Centre Plaza, the Swimming Pool and the Lounge Plaza for the penthouse residents.

The tower's main green feature is the enclosed linked vertical atriums that extend from the ground floor all the way to the roof garden. The sunken plaza with a green landscaped courtyard is located in the middle of the lobby which is connected to another plaza via escalators. A green street system is provided with a tree lined public realm as well as wall hangers and climbing plants. The towers have roof gardens that have a cafeteria for the penthouse dwellers with a swimming pool for the residences.

Legend
1 Site plan
2 View from west
3 Sun path diagram
4 Cross-section
5 View of main entrance
6 View of roof canopy
7 Exterior view
8 View of the façade

5

6

Santa Fe Tower

7

8

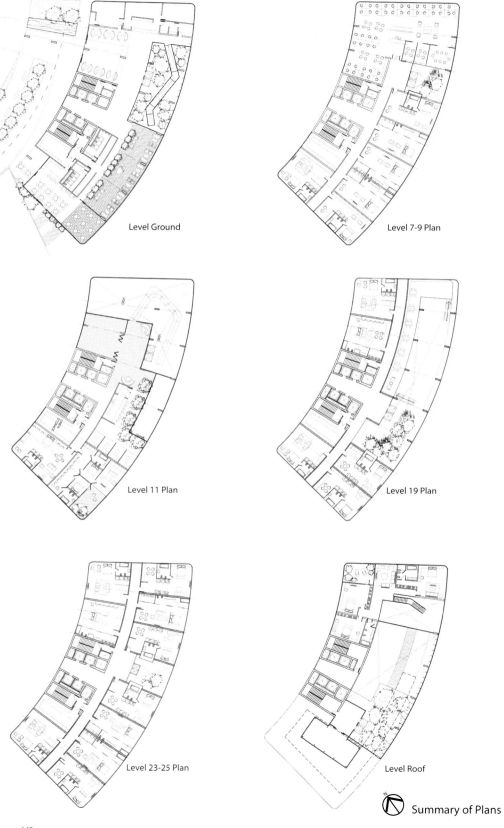

Level Ground

Level 7-9 Plan

Level 11 Plan

Level 19 Plan

Level 23-25 Plan

Level Roof

Summary of Plans

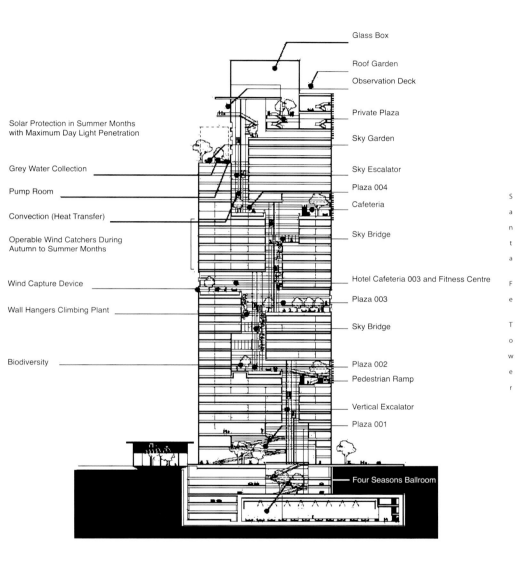

Glass Box

Roof Garden

Observation Deck

Private Plaza

Sky Garden

Solar Protection in Summer Months
with Maximum Day Light Penetration

Grey Water Collection

Sky Escalator

Pump Room

Plaza 004

Cafeteria

Convection (Heat Transfer)

Operable Wind Catchers During
Autumn to Summer Months

Sky Bridge

Wind Capture Device

Hotel Cafeteria 003 and Fitness Centre

Plaza 003

Wall Hangers Climbing Plant

Sky Bridge

Biodiversity

Plaza 002

Pedestrian Ramp

Vertical Excalator

Plaza 001

Four Seasons Ballroom

Santa Fe Tower

Legend

9   Summary of plans

10 Interconnected Series of Enclosed Green Atrium

11

Green Lung

12

Solid/Void

13

Motion/Movement

14

15

16

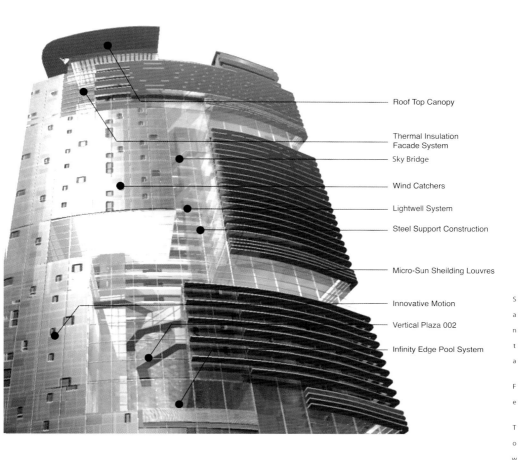

Roof Top Canopy

Thermal Insulation
Facade System

Sky Bridge

Wind Catchers

Lightwell System

Steel Support Construction

Micro-Sun Sheilding Louvres

Innovative Motion

Vertical Plaza 002

Infinity Edge Pool System

Legend

11 Green lung diagram
12 Solid/void diagram
13 Motion/movement diagram
14 External view of enclosed skycourts
15 Internal courtyard with water features
16 Internal atrium
17 Façade

Gnome Research Building Phase 1

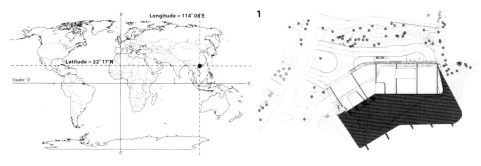

1

Location
Hong Kong

Climatic Zone
Temperate

Vegetation Zone
Rainforest

No. of Storeys
10

Areas
GFA   : 13,300 sq.m.
NFA   : 9,500 sq.m.

Site Area
8,742 sq.m.

Plot Ratio
1 : 5

2

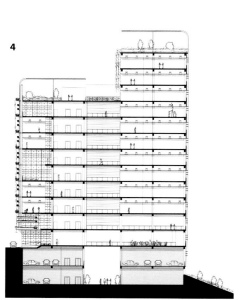

4

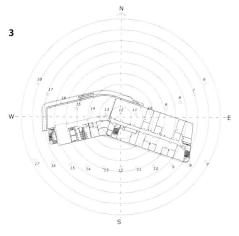

3

The building is to be used for gnome research and to create a unique environment for interdisciplinary exchange. The floors have been designed for maximum laboratory efficiency, using a 3.3 metre grid for standard laboratory furniture and allow for accommodation of evolving needs and technologies. The design maximises open, uninterrupted spaces to allow for flexibility in present layouts and future changes.

The existing trees on the site will be protected and the layout of the new buildings will involve minimal removal of existing trees.

The building's key green feature is a nexus of green planters that extends from the existing park at the rear of the site to the edge of Sassons Road as an ecological corridor connecting all floors to the roof garden. Social zones are provided at the ground plane which consist of a sunken garden, ceremonial plaza, a social garden, a garden walk, a herbal garden, a quiet garden and large trees. There are also interaction spaces to provide opportunities for users to meet for lunch, to share ideas and for informal lecture presentation and open-air conferences.

5

6

8

7

Legend
1 Site plan
2 Worm's eye view
3 Sun path diagram
4 Cross-section
5 Layered steps of planters
6 View from south-west
7 Aerial view from south-east
8 Building in context

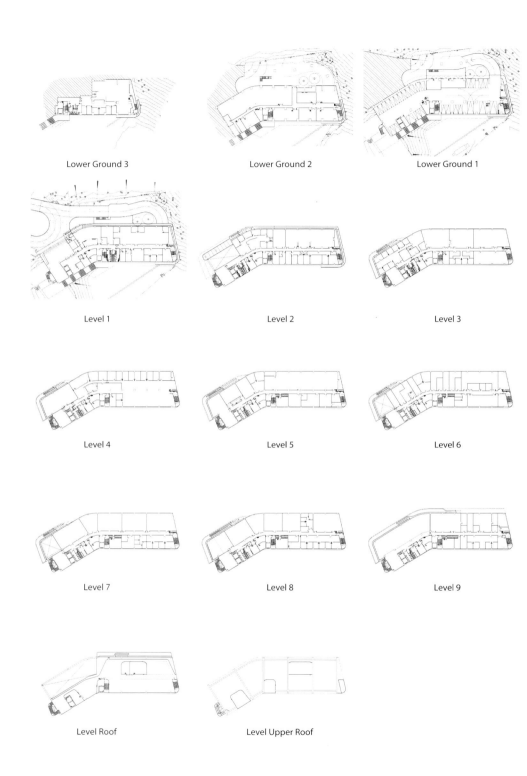

Lower Ground 3

Lower Ground 2

Lower Ground 1

Level 1

Level 2

Level 3

Level 4

Level 5

Level 6

Level 7

Level 8

Level 9

Level Roof

Level Upper Roof

10

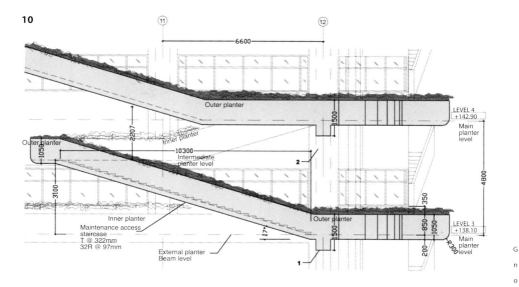

6600

⑪ ⑫

Outer planter

LEVEL 4
+142.90
Main planter level

2207

Inner planter

1050

Outer planter

10300
Intermediate planter level

2

3100

Inner planter

Outer planter

LEVEL 3
+138.10
Main planter level

Maintenance access staircase
T @ 322mm
32R @ 97mm

External planter
Beam level

1

350

850

1050

200

R 300

4900

1500

1500

1. 600 x 650mm (h) External planter beam
2. 600 x 600mm column
3. Column with down pipes both sides

11

12

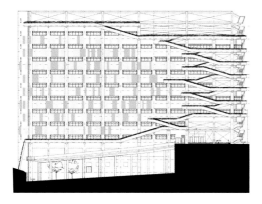

Legend
9 Summary of plans
10 Planter box details
11 Roof top garden
12 North elevation

13

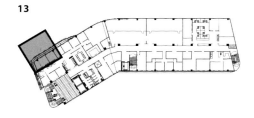

14

15

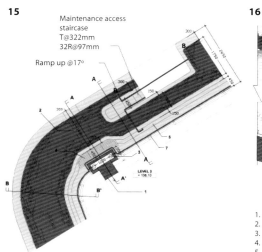

Maintenance access
staircase
T@322mm
32R@97mm

Ramp up @17°

1. 600 x 600mm Column
2. 600 x 650mm External beam
3. 150mm PVC drainage down pipe
4. 1800mm (w) x 150mm (d) scupper drain with m/s grille cover
5. 150mm Scupper drain laid to fall
6. 40mm Safety railing @550mm above planter
7. 40mm Safety railing @900mm
8. 40mm Perforated pipe with geotextile laid @ 3° gradient
9. 2mm Stainless steel safety line supported by hanges

16

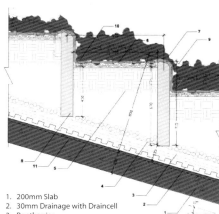

1. 200mm Slab
2. 30mm Drainage with Draincell
3. Rootbarrier
4. 30mm Aggragate
5. 550mm high Planting medium
6. 40mm diameter Irrigation drip pipe
7. 500mm high Proposed vegetation
8. 100mm thk Barrier wall@615mm high
9. Top edge of Planter box
10. Pipe clip
11. Water-proofing membrane

17

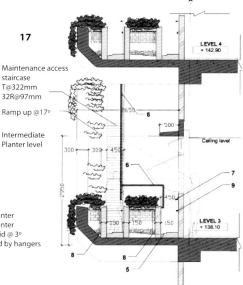

Maintenance access
staircase
T@322mm
32R@97mm

Ramp up @17°

Intermediate
Planter level

5. 150mm Scupper drain laid to fall
6. 40mm Safety railing @ 550mm above planter
7. 40mm Safety railing @ 900mm above planter
8. 40mm Perforated pipe with geotextile laid @ 3°
9. 2mm Stainless steel safety line supported by hangers

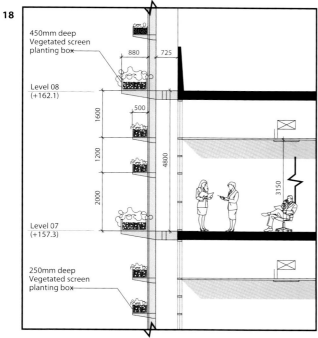

18

450mm deep Vegetated screen planting box

880 725

Level 08 (+162.1)

1600

500

1200

4800

2000

3150

Level 07 (+157.3)

250mm deep Vegetated screen planting box

Detail Section / Vegetated Screen
Scale 1:150

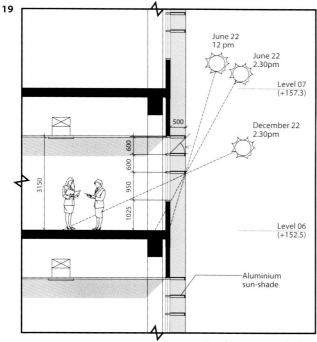

19

June 22 12 pm

June 22 2.30pm

Level 07 (+157.3)

500

December 22 2.30pm

600

600

3150

950

1025

Level 06 (+152.5)

Aluminium sun-shade

Detail Section / Sun-shade
Scale 1:150

Legend

13 Key plan

14 South west-elevation

15 Sectional plan

16 Section B-B

17 Section A-A

18 Detail section: Vegetated screen

19 Detail section: Sunshade

Acknowledgements

Book Coordinator
Nor Azua Ruslan & Siti Azman

Material Compilation by
Nor Azua Ruslan with the assistance of
Siti Azman, Ashley, Amanda, Mohd Hasaludin,

Book Design by
EHT Creative & Graphic Services (Malaysia)

Photography
KL Ng
Albert Lim

Models
Technibuilt
JM Kiang Modeller
Excell Matrix

Notes